WHY GANDHI STILL MATTERS

WHY GANDHI STILL MATTERS

AN APPRAISAL
OF THE MAHATMA'S LEGACY

RAJMOHAN GANDHI

ALEPH

For Tara

ALEPH BOOK COMPANY
An independent publishing firm
promoted by *Rupa Publications India*

First published in India in 2017
by Aleph Book Company
7/16 Ansari Road, Daryaganj
New Delhi 110 002

ISBN: 978-93-86021-15-1

1 3 5 7 9 10 8 6 4 2

Printed and bound in India by
Replika Press Pvt. Ltd, India

CONTENTS

AUTHOR'S NOTE

This book originated in the fall of 2015 during a conversation in Basking Ridge, New Jersey, at the home of good friends Akshay and Anar Shah, where another friend, Dr Barindra Desai, was also present.

As is true for several others from India now living in the United States, the families of Barindra Desai, Akshay Shah and Anar Shah were proud participants in India's freedom movement, embracing long years in prison and other hardships.

During the conversation, Akshay recalled lectures on Gandhi given years earlier at Columbia University by the American scholar Dennis Dalton, adding that Dalton's powerful lectures had drawn standing-room-only audiences, and asked me to offer a fresh series of Gandhi lectures for newer times. His wife Anar and Dr Desai backed the proposal.

Within weeks of my expressing willingness, Sherman Garnett, the dean of James Madison College at Michigan State University (MSU) in East Lansing, invited me, on his university's behalf, to deliver the lectures, which I did in fall 2016.

This book offers, in revised form, the eight lectures given at MSU, plus an additional piece on the author Gandhi. Focusing on Hind Swaraj, this ninth and concluding chapter, The Enduring Truth in his Writings, is based on a paper presented in 2009, exactly a hundred years after Gandhi's famed text was written, at an international conference convened in Delhi by the Centre for the Study of Developing Societies.

Those interested in comparing the text of this book with the MSU lectures, which were recorded by the university on video, should know that The Legacy of Gandhi, the chapter with which this book opens, was at MSU the subject of the eighth and final lecture. Otherwise the book and the lectures observe the same sequence.

I thank Sherman Garnett, Akshay Shah, Anar Shah and Barindra Desai for their roles in this book's emergence.

From his remarkable archive Aditya Arya very kindly provided the photograph used on the back cover. For enthusiastic publishing and helpful suggestions, I thank David Davidar and his talented team at Aleph.

R.G.
Gurgaon
March 2017

WHY GANDHI STILL MATTERS

Is Gandhi of interest to the India and world of today? The year 2017 marks the hundredth year of the Champaran satyagraha, and 2019 will see the 150th anniversary of Gandhi's birth. Do these dates establish Gandhi's relevance for a polarized nation and a violent world?

If Gandhi was all that persons like Einstein and Tagore, Gokhale and Nehru and Patel and Martin Luther King, Jr said he was, and what Barack Obama says he was, then why (it may be asked) was India besmirched by Partition and carnage in 1947?

Also, why do corruption and animosities mark India in 2017? As for nonviolence, can anyone look at Syria and still talk of its applicability?

It says something for a person when his relevance is measured by success or failure in leaving behind a perfect world. In India, Gandhi has been criticized not only for not overcoming all the challenges of his time, including the partition demand, but also for not solving all the problems of our age!

In fact, this interest, two entire generations after his time, in what Gandhi failed to accomplish speaks of what he inspired India to expect of him, which was everything, miracles included. He, too, on his part, claimed that if he were perfect, the world around him would change to his liking. Since it did not, we have proof that he was not perfect. Which is exactly what Gandhi always tried to say.

This short book hopes to present a relevant, fallible, amazing and accessible Gandhi. We can agree that perfection and relevance are not the same thing. A person becomes relevant not by solving all contemporary and future problems (which even God seems unable or unwilling to do) but by offering hints for making life more bearable or interesting, or by showing a way out of a forest.

Gandhi showed Indians how to demand freedom without humiliating themselves as petitioners, and without inviting reprisals on fellow Indians, which was the outcome, often, of the pre-Gandhian method of assassinating the Raj's functionaries.

Relevant or not, Gandhi remains interesting. If nothing else, his contradictions give him appeal. As one of his American friends, E. Stanley Jones, remarked, Gandhi was of East and West, the city and the village, a Hindu influenced by Christianity, simple and shrewd, candid and courteous, serious and playful, humble and assertive. 'While the savour is sweet,' added Jones, 'the preponderating impression he leaves is not sweetness but strength.'

In his final years, a close associate of this lover of the name of Rama was the staunch atheist and fighter for caste equality, Gora (Gopalraju Ramachandra Rao), a Telugu Brahmin. To give another example of Gandhian irony, when Gandhi arrived in Delhi in September 1947 (on the way, so he thought, to carnage-hit Punjab), he stayed in the home of his wealthy friend Ghanshyam Das Birla, but one of the first men he talked with on the day of his arrival— to obtain a true picture of what was happening on the streets of Delhi—was the Communist leader, P. C. Joshi.

Gandhi was to then travel by train from Delhi to Wardha before making another journey, agreed to by Jinnah, to Pakistan. Earlier in the day, the historian Radha Kumud Mookerjee had given Gandhi a copy of his latest book.

This man of action—the man who turned down a plea for a treatise by him on nonviolence by saying, 'Action is my domain'— told his close aide Brij Krishna Chandiwala on the last day of his life, 'Ask Bisen [another aide] to pack Professor Mookerjee's book with my things.'

From both sides of bitter divides, politicians continue to invoke Gandhi. Prime Minister Narendra Modi does so all the time even as opponents charge Modi with driving nails into Gandhi's age-old coffin. Palestinians regularly recall Gandhi's warnings from the late 1930s against flooding Palestine with European Jews, while Israeli Gandhians back Palestinians in nonviolent resistance.

Old Indians can recall the support, surprising to many, given in October 1947 by Gandhi, the nonviolence advocate, for flying Indian soldiers to defend Srinagar, which is what both Sheikh Abdullah and Maharaja Hari Singh had urged. Pakistanis remind India that Gandhi wanted the people's will to prevail in Kashmir too, not merely in Hyderabad and Junagadh.

On the subcontinent or indeed anywhere else, few individuals from the first half of the twentieth century are remembered as frequently as Gandhi. A few years ago, Syrians unhappy with their regime spoke of three Gandhian principles they wanted their resistance to stick to: no sectarianism, no foreign involvement, no violence.

The wisdom of those abandoned principles was emblazoned, in letters of blood and fire, in Syria's subsequent grief-laden story.

Gandhi's flaws too may be seen in this book, including a failure to give sufficient attention to the wishes of his wife, sons and numerous other relatives. This failure was connected in part to the ethos of his times, and in larger part to the all-demanding struggle to which Gandhi felt called. Still, the pain felt by Kasturba, Harilal, and other close ones was all too real.

That the imperfect Gandhi was an utterly astonishing human being also emerges from this book, which seeks to present the historical Gandhi, a Mahatma released from myth and also from the slander provoked by his positions, some of which were decidedly unpopular in orthodox circles.

Can a man as complex as Gandhi, and possessing more than one interesting dimension, be presented in a limited number of pages? This too was a question and a demand, which this book seeks to answer.

The nine chapters of this book may be summarized as follows. The first examines the Gandhi legacy and asks the question, 'Seven decades after his death, what remains of his life and work?' At least three things survive, the opening chapter suggests.

One, satyagraha or the weapon of nonviolent resistance, which several remarkable individuals picked up after him. Two, the spirit he instilled into independent India, or, as some might prefer to think, the residue of that spirit. The third legacy consists of tips from Gandhi for coping with the challenges of a changing and often unjust world.

The second chapter attempts to isolate and identify Gandhi's core passion, the driving force of his life. Was it independence, the expulsion of a hated alien rule? A Hindu Ram Rajya, as some British foes and Indian critics charged? Something else? I should not, in this introduction, anticipate the answer.

A couple of separate if not entirely unconnected questions are asked in the third chapter. How did Gandhi hit upon satyagraha or nonviolent resistance, which was his gift to the world? Secondly, and intriguingly, who or what was Gandhi's God? To what deity or force did Gandhi turn in moments of greatest despair or urgency?

Chapters 4, 5 and 6 are the most 'political' of the nine. Focusing on his relationship with the British Empire, which at the start found Gandhi singing *God Save the Queen* with gusto, Chapter 4 examines in particular the Gandhi-Churchill equation.

The long and testing relationship between the two, which influenced the India-Empire story, originated in the late 1890s in South Africa, where for different reasons the two had found themselves. Gandhi and Churchill were thrown there into lifelong confrontation, though their first face-to-face meeting, which was also their last, took place only in 1906, in London.

Chapter 5 examines Gandhi's valiant and, in the end, unsuccessful attempt to preserve a united India, as also the goals and strategies of Muhammad Ali Jinnah, the fellow-Gujarati who, like Gandhi, studied law in London.

How deeply did Jinnah desire Pakistan? Was Gandhi sufficiently resolute, and sufficiently shrewd, in his strategies to save India's unity? What role did other forces, indigenous and alien, play in the partition outcome? These questions are what Chapter 5 addresses.

The sixth chapter touches upon what perhaps is the most discussed Gandhi-related question in today's India: his stand, or seemingly changing stands, on the caste question, plus his roller-coaster relationship with a foe and partner of extraordinary power, Dr Bhimrao Ambedkar.

The nature, limitations and potency of Gandhi's ahimsa, as also a significant contradiction in it, form the subject of Chapter 7. How an ancient Indian doctrine, blessed in Hinduism, Buddhism and Jainism but sadly reduced to mere rules of diet, became in Gandhi's hands an explosive yet constructive force is the subject of this chapter, which also compares Gandhian nonviolence with Western pacifism.

Also discussed in this seventh chapter is Gandhi's significant regret that while nonviolence was widely accepted as a strategy, many Indians—Hindus, Muslims and others—seemed to regard hatred as a positive value.

Much narrower in the period covered, but possessing a greater personal focus, is Chapter 8, which takes the reader on a journey across the final phase of Gandhi's life, a phase sad in some ways, magnificent in other ways.

The ninth and final chapter is about Gandhi's writings, which are of enduring appeal and constitute a legacy not examined in the opening chapter. A focus in the chapter is on the only theoretical work Gandhi ever wrote: *Hind Swaraj*.

In *Hind Swaraj*, composed on a ship between England and South Africa in 1909, Gandhi theorized the satyagraha that he and his comrades in South Africa had already begun to offer, and pledged his resolve to offer it some day in India.

As is well known, *Hind Swaraj* also questioned the supposed blessings of industrialization and Western civilization. The somewhat unconventional reading presented by me may be of interest to some.

With these remarks, I invite the indulgence, and scrutiny, of readers.

CHAPTER 1

THE LEGACY OF GANDHI

At the start of September 1997, when I arrived in the United States to begin what unexpectedly became a fifteen-year spell of teaching and research at the University of Illinois at Urbana-Champaign, Princess Diana had just died in a car crash. Many were shocked and sad, and not only in Great Britain.

Trying to portray her legacy, television channels in the US showed shots of her sons, fifteen-year-old William and thirteen-year-old Harry—dignified and photogenic, both of them. Looking at them, I thought of the lecture I was expected to give on the legacy of Gandhi, who had died fifty-two years, or almost two generations, earlier.

Even if I possessed their photographs, which I did not, I knew I could not present his fifteen grandchildren, of whom I was one, or the many more great-grandchildren, and say, 'Look, here is Gandhi's legacy.' That would not have worked, even though, if you ask me, certainly the *great*-grandchildren, and *their* children, are quite dignified and photogenic.

Descendants would not fit the bill in part because 'family first' was *not* Gandhi's motto. Cheated for long by big men who nourished the ambitions of favourite offspring, the people of India honoured Gandhi because his family did *not* come first with him. Steering Ship India across dangerous waters, Captain Gandhi did not save the best lifeboats for his family.

Saying that in him 'divine providence ha[d] given [India] a

burning thunderbolt of shakti', Gandhi's great friend and occasional critic, the poet Tagore, would add: Gandhi 'stopped at the threshold of huts of thousands of the dispossessed, like one of their own... spoke in their own language... and won the heart of India with his love.'

Raised in a privileged family in Rajkot in western India, Mohan had learnt as a boy to recite the family pedigree, of which he was proud. When he was in his seventies, the hugs that Gandhi gave his grandchildren revealed his love for them, the flesh of his flesh.

Yet many thought that the star of destiny that pulled Gandhi like a magnet and drove him to serve the Indian people distanced Gandhi from his biological family while bonding him with countless Indians who seemed to need him even more than his sons and grandchildren.

They thought that the relationship between Gandhi and his sons, daughters-in-law, and grandchildren was detached, disengaged, perhaps even cold. This was indicated to me, for example, by the legendary Aruna Asaf Ali, shortly before her death in 1996.

Aruna is a celebrated figure in India's liberation story, a well-connected Bengali Brahmin whose brother had married Tagore's daughter Mira. Aruna herself had married a Muslim lawyer and independence activist from north India, Asaf Ali. She went underground during Quit India, became a hero, and fought until the day she died for equality and human rights.

Not long before her death, Aruna and others, including my brother Ramchandra, better known as Ramu Gandhi the philosopher, all of them concerned about challenges to India's pluralism, met at the Tees January Marg house in New Delhi where Gandhi had been assassinated fifty years earlier. To those gathered, Ramu, now deceased, spoke feelingly of our grandfather's last days. Listening to him, Aruna turned to me and said:

'I had no idea Ramu felt so deeply about Bapu's assassination.'

Well, he did, along with a great many others. Aruna was not alone in thinking that the relationship between Gandhi and his children and grandchildren was exactly like his relationship with every Indian.

It was, and it was not. Blood brought something extra.

We deeply loved our grandfather, because of the kind of person he was, and because, despite the rarity and brevity of our times with him, a rarity and brevity connected to his prison-going and his involvement with countless people, he was an affectionate grandfather.

Since our father, Devadas, Gandhi's youngest son, was based in Delhi, editing the largest newspaper there, my siblings and I saw a good deal of our grandfather while he spent chunks of his final years in Delhi.

We bantered with him walking to and back from his 5 p.m. prayer meetings in the Dalit settlement where he often stayed, or on the Birla House lawns on what is now Tees January Marg, and on rare occasions we had one-on-one exchanges, as when he mocked a new pair of spectacles I was wearing while visiting him in the Balmiki Colony of Dalits on Mandir Marg.

Aware of his love of thrift, I was hoping he would not notice the new object on my face, but the old man was sharp. 'You have something new on your nose,' he said. I was ready to fight back. 'You know I have weak eyes,' I told him, 'I needed the new spectacles.' 'And you also needed a new frame?' he asked.

One-on-one times were rare because in this final phase of his life, when freedom, partition, violence, and migrations descended simultaneously on India, Gandhi's hours and minutes were above all devoted to victims of violence—Hindu, Sikh and Muslim victims— some of whom joined his multi-faith prayer meetings.

Being often present at these, I saw how my grandfather responded when, as happened on occasion, an angry Hindu, or more than one, objected to the recitation of the Quran's short opening chapter, Al-Fatiha. Surprised at his patience with the protesters, I would also at times wonder whether one day they would physically attack my grandfather, whose chest was barely protected with clothes, and who had no bodyguard.

Though telling myself that I should try to protect him, I was not present on the fateful day, 30 January 1948, when he was killed.

Twelve-and-a-half at the time, I was taking part in a school athletics event.

Gandhi often appears in my dreams. There was a period about twenty years ago, that is, more than forty years after he was gone, when in several consecutive dreams I searched in different parts of Delhi for him, until to my unspeakable joy I found that he was alive, staying with one or two companions in a tiny but clean box-like shack on Panchkuian Road in New Delhi, not far from Paharganj, the sort of shack that refugees from West Punjab had used in 1947 and for some years thereafter.

The dream where I had found him appeared at least twice, felt utterly real, and was hard to shake off.

He loved his grandchildren and we loved him, but there was no question of his belonging only to us. The fact that the people of India possessed him, owned him, was a given. It was accepted. It made no difference to our feeling for him.

That fact greatly weakens any case for identifying Gandhi's descendants as a major part of his legacy. For that we must go elsewhere. Before leaving the descendants, however, let me say in all fairness that his four sons and four daughters-in-law (there were no daughters, sadly), the fifteen grandchildren, of whom seven are still alive (four females and three males), and more numerous great-grandchildren, have between them contributed well and honourably to the intellectual, social and political life of India, and also of South Africa, Great Britain and the United States.

■

To my mind, three things constitute the Gandhi legacy: nonviolence as a weapon of struggle, the independent nation of India, and signposts for life today anywhere on earth.

As for nonviolence, I will speak of five famous persons who picked up that weapon after Gandhi and went on to wield it with compelling power.

Many others, we know, have also used that weapon. Thousands

more use it without our knowledge, and most of them without any remembrance of Gandhi. In situations big and small, women and men daily strive for justice without violence or hate, adding to our world's stock of goodness. These not-so-famous women and men are the people whose deeds around us—in our neighbourhood, perhaps even in our families—keep our spirits going.

Let us think of such persons as I speak of Khan Abdul Ghaffar Khan, Nelson Mandela, Martin Luther King, Jr, the Dalai Lama, and Aung San Suu Kyi, to name them in the order of their birth. All five are persons I have had the privilege of meeting and in some cases of knowing!

Ghaffar Khan (1890-1988), a Sunni Muslim from the subcontinent's Northwest Frontier Province, a Pashtun whom the British imprisoned for twelve years and Pakistani rulers for fifteen years, was, as I said in the biography I wrote of him, 'an immensely tall figure with an absolutely straight back, a great nose, kindly eyes, and a permanent aura of non-violent defiance'.

I was ten years old when I first saw Ghaffar Khan in 1945, when he and his older brother Khan Abdul Jabbar Khan, better known as Dr Khan Sahib, stayed for a few days in our home, a second-floor apartment in what used to be called Connaught Circus in New Delhi. I saw him last in 1987 in Bombay's Raj Bhavan (the mansion of the Maharashtra governor) when he was almost ninety-seven.

His people called him Badshah Khan or Bacha Khan, meaning 'King' Khan. Independence from foreign rule was one fire in his soul. Another of his passions was to end the revenge code to which his Pashtun people were sworn.

Moreover, non-Muslims were as important as Muslims to Badshah Khan, who declared in the late 1940s that he and his Pashtuns would protect the small population of Hindus, Sikhs and Christians living in the overwhelmingly Muslim Northwest Frontier Province (NWFP).

Enthusiastic about his region's Buddhist history, this devout Muslim who had exiled himself to Afghanistan in the mid-1960s would proudly take Hindu visitors from India to Bamiyan to show them the great Buddha statues (which the Taliban detonated and demolished in March 2001).

Wanting Pashtun women to study, work and lead, Ghaffar Khan in 1932 sent his daughter Mehr Taj, when she had barely entered her teens, to study in England, and to the US he sent his son Abdul Ghani Khan, who would become a famed painter, sculptor and poet.

To change Pashtun society and fight non-violently for Indian independence, Ghaffar Khan founded the Khudai Khidmatgars, or volunteering 'servants of God', in 1929. In the following year, as part of the campaign triggered by Gandhi's Salt March, these Khudai Khidmatgars, known also as the Red Shirts, allied with the Indian National Congress and faced the Empire's armed and mounted police, but refused to back down or hit back.

It was an epic moment in India's freedom movement.

Seven years later, in 1937, the Khudai Khidmatgars were voted to power in the NWFP. Badshah Khan's older brother, Dr Khan Sahib, became the province's prime minister. Ghaffar Khan's son Ghani Khan would later recall a conversation with an Englishman, a military and political officer called Colonel R. N. Bacon, who had confronted the Red Shirts in that classic struggle of 1930:

> [Bacon] told me, 'Ghani, I was the Assistant Commissioner in Charsadda. The Red Shirts would be brought to me. I had orders to give them each two years rigorous imprisonment. I would say, "Are you a Red Shirt?" They would say yes. "Do you want freedom?" "Yes, I want freedom." "If I release you, will you do it again?" "Yes."'
>
> [Bacon] said, 'I would want to get up and hug him. Instead I would write, "Two years."'

In 1939, Ghaffar Khan would recall:

> The sight of an Englishman [used to] frighten us. [Our] movement has instilled fresh life into us... We have shed our fear and are no longer afraid of an Englishman or for that

matter of any man. Englishmen are afraid of our nonviolence. A nonviolent [Pashtun], they say, is more dangerous than a violent [Pashtun].

Remembering violent upheavals in the 1890s that crippled life in the NWFP during his boyhood, Ghaffar Khan would speak of the superior results of his movements:

The British crushed the violent movement in no time... If a Britisher was killed, not only [was] the culprit...punished, but the whole village and entire region suffered for it. The people held the violence and its doer responsible for the repression. In the nonviolent movement, *we* courted suffering, and the community did not suffer but benefited. Thus it won [the] love and sympathy of the people.

Seasoned imperialists like Sir Reginald Coupland assumed, in Coupland's words, that nonviolence would be 'almost unintelligible on the Frontier where most men carry firearms and the maintenance of the blood-feud is still regarded as a sacred duty'.

It was said that a male Pashtun baby arrived in this world with a rifle or sword in his hand. But when Ghaffar Khan asked Pashtuns to shed all weapons and join a nonviolent struggle against the Empire, they began to question their destructive blood feuds, handed down from father to son.

Visiting the Frontier in the 1930s, Halide Edib Adivar, the Turkish writer, found what she called 'a new interpretation of force'. To her, this demonstration of nonviolent force, 'coming from strong and fearless men,' was 'very unexpected'. It was achieved by Ghaffar Khan's success in linking nonviolence to Islam.

Writing seven decades later, in 2003, the commentator Harold Gould contrasted the methods of Gandhi and Ghaffar Khan which, in Gould's words, 'brought down empires' in South Asia, with the 'walking bombs' in the Middle East and Kashmir 'whose self-detonations invite devastating retaliatory assaults on their innocent fellow citizens'.

Accused by pro-Empire Pashtuns of associating with idol-worshipping Hindus, Ghaffar Khan responded with these words:

> If they are idol worshippers, what are we? What is the worship of tombs? How are [the Hindus] any the less devotees of God when I know that they believe in one God? And why do you despair of Hindu-Muslim unity? Look at the fields over there. The grain sowed there has to remain in the earth for a certain time, then it sprouts and in due time yields hundreds of its kind. The same is the case about every effort in a good cause.

Here is what Ghaffar Khan said in May 1947 in Shabqadar in the heart of the Pashtun country:

> Some people mislead you in the name of Islam. I feel it is my duty to warn you against future dangers so that I may justify myself before man and God on the Day of Judgement... I warn [my extremist] brethren that the fire they kindle will spread in wild blaze and consume everything in its way.

His Pashtuns frequently failed to heed their Badshah Khan. Persisting with mutual jealousies, they allowed themselves to be misled. Still, they loved Badshah Khan as they had not, for decades, loved another Pashtun. Every new incarceration or exile of his only increased this love, which at his death in 1988 took the shape of an unforgettable pageant across the Khyber, from Peshawar to Jalalabad, with all sides in that region's seemingly unending conflicts silencing their guns for his final rites.

■

It was in the early summer of 1957 that I made my first trip to the US, during which I was able to meet Martin Luther King, Jr. In fact, I had two meetings with him, each very brief, in Washington DC. One was when along with a couple of friends I was trying to cross a street. From the opposite side emerged this quiet, serious young person. One of my companions mumbled something about me to him, I shook his friendly hand, and MLK Jr continued on his way.

That summer in 1957, though not yet as famous as he would shortly become, he received an award in Washington DC. When the award was given to him, I met him for a second time. Someone took a photograph. In this picture MLK Jr. is only twenty-eight, I am just under twenty-two.

That was my last encounter with him. Shortly afterwards I had a much longer conversation, in Atlanta, Georgia, with his father, Martin Luther King, or Daddy King as he was called. Outwardly, father and son provided a sharp contrast: Daddy King was outspoken, vigorous, and combative; his son was gentle, quiet, and at times seemingly passive.

But there was a fire in his soul. We all know how that fire brought consciences to life all over the world.

In February 1959, twenty months after my brief encounters with him, Dr King visited India. On his return, he offered an assessment of Gandhi and of nonviolent struggle in a sermon at the Dexter Avenue Baptist Church in Montgomery, Alabama. Every student of nonviolence, Gandhi or King should read this remarkable sermon on 22 March 1959 by King who had just turned thirty. Here I will quote only a sentence from it.

[Gandhi] was able to achieve for his people independence from the domination of the British Empire without lifting one gun or without uttering one curse word.

Four years later, in 1963, Dr King led a march on Washington and delivered his 'I Have a Dream' speech. The Civil Rights Act came into being in 1964, and in 1965, after brutalities during the march led by Dr King from Selma to Montgomery, America's Blacks won the historic Voting Rights Act.

How did King first hear about Gandhi? In 1950, two years after Gandhi's assassination, twenty-year-old, Martin—or Mike, as he was called then—went to Friendship House in Philadelphia to hear a talk on Gandhi by Dr Mordecai Johnson, president of Howard University.

We have King's own words. '[Dr. Johnson's] message was so profound and electrifying that I left the meeting and bought a half-dozen books on Gandhi's life and works'.

Absorbing the books, King thought that Gandhi had shown a way both moral and practical for oppressed people to fight injustice. King, to use his words, saw Gandhi as 'lift[ing] the love ethic of Jesus above mere interaction between individuals to a powerful, effective social force on a large scale'.

In 1936 Gandhi met with four African Americans: Howard Thurman, then dean of Rankin Chapel at Howard University in Washington DC, his wife, Sue Bailey Thurman, and the Thurmans' friends, Edward and Phenola Carroll, sincere Christians all of them.

It was at this 1936 meeting in Bardoli, western India, with the Thurmans and the Carrolls that Gandhi made what in the light of later history was clearly a prophetic remark.

> Well, if it comes true, it may be through the [African Americans]
> that the unadulterated message of nonviolence will be delivered
> to the world.

This farsighted remark was the product of reflection, and interaction— interaction with Howard Thurman and his friends, and earlier interactions, starting in 1893 in South Africa, with a remarkable sequence of African Americans.

Martin was just seven in 1936, but the forces of destiny that would catapult King and make him the symbol of nonviolent resistance all over the world, including in what for decades was the Soviet empire, were already at work.

■

While he died forty-three years *after* King was assassinated, Nelson Mandela was born in 1918, eleven years *before* King's birth. When Mandela first visited India in 1990, it was within months of his release from almost three decades of imprisonment.

He was not yet South Africa's president. The long-standing ban on the party to which he belonged, the African National Congress, had only just been lifted. Much of apartheid was still in place, and the ANC remained a fighting machine.

In 1990, Gandhi had been dead for forty-two years. Mandela was seventy-two. I was fifty-five and a member of the Rajya Sabha.

The Indian government honoured Mandela with the country's highest honour, the Bharat Ratna. A small plane was put at Mandela's disposal for seeing India. He chose to visit Agra, where the Taj Mahal is located, Benares or Varanasi, the holy city of the Hindus, and Calcutta or Kolkata, the large city in eastern India from which the British once governed much of Asia.

I asked for and obtained the opportunity to accompany the future president and Nobel laureate to these places. I saw his extraordinary courtesy to innumerable autograph seekers. Some didn't even bring books or notebooks—they just shoved pieces of paper under his nose. Carefully, painstakingly, he wrote out first their names, then the words 'With best wishes,' and finally, in a clear, legible hand, 'Nelson R. Mandela'—adding the date.

Inside the plane, when he was free from Indian crowds and could focus on South African matters, I saw the ANC commander in action, giving crisp, concise instructions to four key lieutenants travelling with him.

In Varanasi, on a boat in the sacred river Ganga, Mandela was the keenly curious student of cultures, straining his neck in every direction to see if any dead bodies were bobbing up in the water—he knew that Hindus attached great value to dying in Benares and consigning the body into the sacred Ganga.

In Calcutta, where he spent two nights in the grand house built in 1803 for the Empire's chief guardian, I observed Mandela's interest in the ordinary person. As he was leaving this mansion, Mandela sought out the servants who worked there, many of whom had confined themselves to unlit interior spaces.

These employees were shy, and tradition had instructed them

to remain anonymous. But Mandela went down the mansion's long corridors in search of them, drew them forward, shook hands with them, and thanked them.

Towards the end of his India visit, I anchored a television programme where a dozen or so young Indians asked Mandela questions. One of them, recalling that Mayor Dinkins of New York City had described Mandela as the Moses of his people, asked, 'How does Mandela describe himself?'

Mandela's immediate answer was: 'Let me tell you about Oliver Tambo, president of the African National Congress.'

A focus on himself did not interest Mandela. He was drawn more to the battles he had to fight and to his teammates in those battles.

Before his almost endless incarceration, Mandela, along with his companions, had used lethal weapons in his struggle, something that Gandhi and King had never done.

Alike, however, in embracing struggle, Gandhi, Mandela and King were also alike in embracing reconciliation. When we consider the decades of apartheid and imprisonment he endured, Mandela astonishes us with his large, healed, and welcoming heart.

Like King's America and Gandhi's India, Mandela's South Africa was a home for *all* its residents.

On that 1990 visit, India's president, R. Venkataraman, told Mandela that he would be praying for him as he faced the tough days that lay ahead. 'Thank you, Mr President,' said Mandela, adding, 'And please pray also for Mr de Klerk.' Frederik Willem de Klerk was then the white president of a South Africa in transition.

■

When he made his dramatic escape from Tibet in 1959, the Dalai Lama was only twenty-four. That year I met him for the first time and noticed his curiosity about the whole wide world and also about cameras that could capture the world's wonder.

I have met him more than a dozen times in the nearly sixty years since. From the early years of his exile, I have marvelled at the

Dalai Lama's ability to invite the world's attention to Tibet when he cannot even set foot on his homeland.

He and his followers in exile, a people without a land, have stirred consciences all over the world not for a month, or a year, but year after year for six decades!

Other peoples battle from their soil for self-determination and freedom, but often the world loses interest in their struggles. One reason for the Dalai Lama's success is his nonviolence, and a second reason is his interest in every person he meets.

Since his struggle has been a very long one, many have met him more than once. I have personally observed the Dalai Lama's extraordinary ability to recall facts about persons he is meeting after a gap of several years. Why wouldn't the world love one who really seems to love all the world's people?

The Dalai Lama is also very human. I have heard him speak of his deep disappointment that the government of China does not trust him or the Tibetan people, and also of his sadness that China's power silences many people in the world. But the Dalai Lama takes the long view, and he is aware that growing numbers of Chinese respect and admire him. And I know from personal knowledge of *his* warmth for the people of China.

That he wishes to retain ties with China is public knowledge. Again and again the Dalai Lama has declared that his nonviolent struggle for equality and autonomy is for a Tibet connected to China.

■

Unlike her fellow-Buddhist and fellow-Nobel laureate, the Dalai Lama, Aung San Suu Kyi, or Daw Suu Kyi as Burma's people call her, has witnessed at least a partial realization of her dreams. After long spells of imprisonment or house arrest, she is now the elected leader of her people, even if she cannot be called president.

Both the Dalai Lama and Aung San Suu Kyi acknowledge a debt and a link to Gandhi. When the Dalai Lama received the Nobel Peace Prize in 1989, he said, 'I accept [the prize] as a tribute to the man who founded the modern tradition of nonviolent action for change—Mahatma Gandhi—whose life taught and inspired me.'

Two years later, in 1991, when Aung San Suu Kyi was awarded, while in detention, *her* Nobel, she was represented by her husband Michael Aris, who would die in 1999, and by their sons Alexander and Kim. The committee selecting her for the award spoke of her commitment to democracy, nonviolence, human rights, and ethnic conciliation, of how Gandhi had inspired her, and added: 'It is our hope that Aung San Suu Kyi will see her struggle crowned with success.'

After more years of house arrest, she was released in 1995, with severe restrictions. Shortly after this 'release', Alan Clements, an American Buddhist, interviewed her a few times over a period of months. He posed a question given by a Rangoon University student: 'Should Burma's democracy movement engage in an armed struggle rather than continuing in a non-violent way?' Replied Suu Kyi:

> Even if the democracy movement were to succeed through force of arms, it would leave in the minds of the people the idea that whoever has greater armed might wins in the end. [Non-violence] is often the slower way and I understand why our young people feel that non-violence will not work, especially when the authorities in Burma are prepared to talk to insurgent groups but not to an organization like the NLD [National League for Democracy] which carries no arms... But I cannot encourage that kind of attitude. Because if we do, we will be perpetuating a cycle of violence that will never come to an end.

When Clements asked if she was a 'good' person, Suu Kyi replied:

> I do try to be good *(laughs)*. That is the way my mother brought me up... I'm not saying that I succeed all the time but I do try. I have a terrible temper. I will say that I don't get as angry now as I used to... But when I think somebody

has been hypocritical or unjust, I have to confess that I still get very angry... When I get really angry, I...say to myself, well, I'm angry, I'm angry, I've got to control this anger. And that brings it under control to a certain extent.

Asked if Burma's generals had managed to control her emotionally or mentally, Daw Suu Kyi replied with words that recall Gandhi's insight:

No, and I think this is because I have never learned to hate them. If I had, I would have really been at their mercy... People ask me why I was not frightened of them... Because I was not aware that they could do whatever they wanted to me? I was fully aware of that. I think it was because I did not hate them, and you cannot really be frightened of people you do not hate. Hate and fear go hand-in-hand.

Observing that 'because of the tremendous repression to which we have been subjected' her struggle needed a spiritual component, Suu Kyi added that her love of literature too was of assistance. 'My other passion is literature, but it seems to dovetail with politics,' she said.

As 1997 was about to arrive, the year when India would mark fifty years of freedom, I requested a keynote from Aung San Suu Kyi for a conference I was helping to organize. Though living under restrictions, she faxed a statement that arrived on the morning of 1 January, bearing a handwritten message, 'Happy New Year'. In her statement, she said:

Many countries have achieved self-government only to find that the rights and freedom of their people have come under greater restraint than in the days when they were ruled by an alien power...

In Burma despite half a century of self-government, good government is still somewhere in the nebulous future. As Gandhiji wrote, 'In truth, a Government that is ideal governs the least. It is no self-government that leaves nothing for the people to do. That is pupillage—our present stage.'

These words were written in 1925, yet could well be applied to the state of present-day Burma, although it might be questioned whether 'pupilage' is not too tender a word to describe the abject situation in which my country finds itself today under a military administration that leaves people with no role to play in their own government. We remain a nation in bondage after forty-nine years of independence...

Then she again quoted Gandhi:

Real Swaraj will come not by the acquisition of authority by a few but by the acquisition of the capacity by all to resist authority when it is abused.

That message was sent in 1997. I last met Aung San Suu Kyi in December 2014, shortly before the elections that would make her the leader of the Burmese people.

The eyes of her friends are on Aung San Suu Kyi, and their prayers are with her, as she cuts a path through the tricky forest of a multi-ethnic Burma which is still largely under army rule, and faces difficult ethnic divides, towards a future of dignity and partnership for all its inhabitants, Buddhist, Christian, Hindu, Muslim or whatever.

■

The independent nation of India also constitutes Gandhi's legacy. George Washington refused to become America's continuing president but will always be associated with American independence. Gandhi was perhaps the only leader of the twentieth century's liberation movements in Asia, Africa and the Middle East not to assume power at independence, but India's independence will always be joined to Gandhi.

Twenty-seven years before his death, during a fascinating debate with Tagore, Gandhi described the texture of his nationalism:

I do not want my house to be walled in on all sides and my windows to be stuffed. I want the culture of all lands to be blown about my house as freely as possible. But I refuse to be blown off my feet by any.

In other parts of the world, the Mexican poet Octavio Paz pointed out, violent wars for independence had often become 'breeding grounds for warlords' and for 'militarism, coups, uprisings, and civil wars'. In India, the nonviolent movement for independence and Gandhi's unconcern with personal power helped produce democracy.

Everyone knows that independent India's imperfections are numerous and profound, yet it is also true that the country has remained democratic all these sixty-nine years; the Indian state possesses a pro-poor tilt; and under the law at least all of India's inhabitants enjoy equal protection from the state.

These positive features owe a good deal to Gandhi's lifelong efforts. The text of India's Constitution was completed twenty-two months after Gandhi's death, but its essential features—democracy, equality, secularism and pluralism—had become national pledges before Gandhi's death, pledges summoned in large part by Gandhi's exertions.

If India alters its Constitution and becomes a Hindu Rashtra, the Hindu State demanded by a small but passionate minority, that would certainly demolish a major pillar of Gandhi's legacy. This threat is not wholly unreal.

Moreover, the Indian state's embrace of nuclear weapons; the widespread worship in Indian society of the god of money; the continuing recourse to violence to settle disputes and bully the vulnerable, including Dalit women and men and Adivasis; inaction from the government when coercive groups threaten dissenters; the harshness in Indian prisons and in institutions like homes for the mentally unwell—all too real features like these have to be seen as a rejection of Gandhi's teachings.

Still, what both state and society in India have absorbed from Gandhi is not insignificant. He inspires struggles in India against corruption and injustice, for the environment and for human rights, struggles often waged in India in Gandhi's name, and from venues linked to Gandhi's battles.

India will remain a crucial site where Gandhi's legacy is either protected and augmented, or damaged and diminished.

Starting with the early 1990s, India has shown impressive economic progress. Hundreds of millions have crossed from poverty to a decent life, but other hundreds of millions remain in distress.

In 1929, shortly before the Salt March for independence, the American thinker, John Mott, asked Gandhi what weighed most on his mind. In his response Gandhi spoke not of alien rule but of

> Our apathy and hardness of heart, if I may use the Biblical phrase...towards the masses and their poverty.

■

Guideposts for our lives today, the third part of the Gandhi legacy, are available from how he lived his life and also from thoughts he spelt out. When we study the life of the man, an imperfect, flawed man, as he would be the first to point out, the man who famously said, 'My life is my message,' we find an unceasing attempt to

- turn the searchlight inwards,
- reach great goals for his people rather than find personal comfort or pleasure,
- strengthen his team, and
- make the vulnerable his priority.

In him, we also find someone

- who puts his life on the line for his beliefs, including the belief that all human beings are equal, and that humanity's God, though differently-addressed, is One and the Same;
- who is as comfortable with 'Truth is God' as with 'God is Truth';
- who successfully taught large numbers that revenge was

both futile and folly;

• and who, born into a family of prestige and proceeding to command unprecedented influence in his large country, died cheerfully with these worldly possessions:

> a pocket watch, a pair of wooden sandals, a pair of spectacles, a wooden bowl for taking his nourishments, and, gifted by a Japanese friend, three tiny porcelain monkeys who seemed to say, 'See no evil, hear no evil, and speak no evil.'

Someone, in short, whose life is his message. It is not a minor legacy.

As for what he said or wrote, let me end by randomly picking, out of a large pool, four quotations. You can decide whether they are relevant.

In a speech in Johannesburg on 18 May 1908, Gandhi named the Africans, the Indians, the Chinese, the so-called Coloured (or mixed) race, and the whites living in South Africa, claimed he had studied the interracial question, and concluded:

> If we look into the future, is it not a heritage we have to leave to posterity, that all the different races commingle and produce a civilization that perhaps the world has not yet seen?

That vision of a commingled humanity was offered 108 years ago. Next, here is Gandhi speaking in 1928—eighty-nine years ago—of what human beings unwilling to restrain themselves can do to Planet Earth, even when they are Indian:

> God forbid that India should take to industrialization after the manner of the West. The economic impact of one single tiny island kingdom today is keeping the world in chains. If an entire nation of three hundred million took to similar economic exploitation, it would strip the world bare like locusts.

The third quote is his diagnosis for splits and divisions, offered a month before independence to a group of politicians:

> As soon as we differ from somebody ever so slightly, or
> a misunderstanding arises, instead of meeting the person
> concerned and trying to find a solution, we take him to task
> publicly. This creates...antagonism...[and] parties and isms.

Finally, eighteen days before his death Gandhi repeated what he had
said numberless times in his life: since they shared the same ground,
India's Hindus and Muslims had to learn to live together.

Doing so, they would help the world, which, like India, holds
people of many faiths: Christians, Muslims, Jews, Hindus, Buddhists,
Jains, Sikhs and others, including atheists.

Conversely, if Indians did not learn to live together, then, in
Gandhi's words of 12 January 1948,

> The loss of her soul by India will mean the loss of the hope
> of the aching, storm-tossed and hungry world.

CHAPTER 2

GANDHI'S PASSIONS

Many decades ago, back in 1948, when Gandhi was killed by an assassin's bullets, the world responded with shock, grief and tribute. Today, seventy years later, he continues to be referred to in all sorts of places.

Why does the world take notice of Gandhi?

A clue may lie in what Albert Einstein said in 1939, nine years before Gandhi's death and eight years before India's independence.

> A leader of his people, unsupported by any outside authority: a politician whose success rests not upon craft nor the mastery of technical devices, but simply on the convincing power of his personality; a victorious fighter who has always scorned the use of force; a man of wisdom and humility, armed with resolve and inflexible consistency, who has devoted all his strength to the uplifting of his people and the betterment of their lot; a man who has confronted the brutality of Europe with the dignity of the simple human being, and thus at all times risen superior.
>
> Generations to come, it may be, will scarce believe that such a one as this ever in flesh and blood walked upon this earth.

These lines can be found in Einstein's book, *Out of My Later Years,* published in New York in 1950. Mark the absence of any reference to India. The Einstein of 1939, the year when Germany attacked Poland, sees Gandhi as a resident of Planet Earth. Yes, he situates

Gandhi against a Europe that had conquered far continents and ruled over vast populations.

■

What was the dominant passion of so singular a person?

Many of Gandhi's imperial opponents were sure that driving the British out was Gandhi's primary if not sole goal. Thus Penderel Moon, the Punjab-based civil servant who became one of the Empire's leading historians, would write:

> The deliverance of India from British rule, which admittedly was Gandhi's chief political aim, would appear also to have been the dominant purpose of his life. He himself would have denied this.

Aware of Gandhi's involvement in social, economic and moral questions, men like Moon and Lord Wavell, India's viceroy from 1943 to 1947 (whose papers Moon edited), called that involvement window-dressing. Denying the evidence of Gandhi's lack of interest in money or in office, they called him a hypocrite.

Wavell wrote in 1946 that he felt anti-British 'malevolence' in Gandhi and that Gandhi's goal was 'the establishment of a Hindu Raj'.

Today, however, a Gandhi statue stands next to the British Parliament, and people in London, New York, Beijing, Tokyo, Cape Town, Nairobi, Canberra, Ottawa, Islamabad and elsewhere associate Gandhi not with a dislike of races, nations or faith communities differing from his, but with the idea that humanity is one, and that we should be the change we wish to see.

■

In the India of today, with its population of 1.2 billion, and perhaps elsewhere too, the following pictures or words seem synonymous with Gandhi:

> One, the pocket watch that always hung from his waist.

Two, a simple pair of eye-glasses under a bald head.

Three, a broom that cleans.

Four, the charkha or the spinning wheel.

Five, a pinch of salt.

Six, 'Vaishnava Jana', the song by the fifteenth-century Gujarati poet Narsi Mehta, defining a good person as someone who feels a stranger's pain.

Seven, an ancient line from an unknown author declaring that Ishwar and Allah refer to the same God; and also, yes,

Eight, the call addressed to the British in 1942, 'Quit India!'

This Quit India Gandhi is suggested I think by the Gandhi holding a walking stick, what Indians call a lathi, which is the Gandhi seen in many places in India, including as the vanguard in the Gyara Murti constellation in New Delhi.

If we reflect on these Gandhi symbols, perhaps we may get to know what drove him.

Let's start with the Quit India call. There is no doubt that the world saw him as a champion for the dignity, equality, and independence of peoples lorded over by others.

In 1921, when under Gandhi's lead the campaign of Non-Cooperation with the Empire was sweeping across India, Marcus Garvey, who was leading a fight in the United States for African Americans, cabled his support for the campaign. In August of that same year, *The Crisis*, the journal edited by the African-American thinker W. E. B. Du Bois, published the entire text of Gandhi's 'Open Letter' addressed that year 'To Every Briton in India'.

After Gandhi's famous arrest and trial in the following year, *The Crisis* wrote: 'White Christianity stood before Gandhi the other day and, let us all confess, cut a sorry figure'. Seven years later, in 1929, *The Crisis* published on its front page a signed message from Gandhi, perhaps the first he addressed directly to American Blacks:

Let not the 12 million [African Americans] be ashamed of the fact that they are the grandchildren of slaves. There is no dishonour in being slaves. There is dishonour in being slave-owners.

Three years later, in 1932, an editorial in the African-American newspaper, the *Chicago Defender,* said:

> What we need in America is a Gandhi who will fight the cause of the oppressed. One who, like Gandhi, can divorce himself from the greed for gold, one who can appreciate the misery of the oppressed.

The *Chicago Defender* had identified the *quality* of Gandhi's fight. All over the world people knew that Gandhi was fighting racial domination, and they also instinctively understood what Einstein would point out: Gandhi was showing that in dignity the oppressed could rise superior to the oppressor.

Throughout his life, moreover, Gandhi seemed to be as firmly opposed to wrongs committed by and among Indians as he was to the Empire's high-handedness. Look, for instance, at his trek in the winter of 1946-47 across the Noakhali area, now part of Bangladesh, where minority Hindus had faced death, rapes and forcible conversion at the hands of the Muslim majority.

On this journey, much of it conducted on foot, Gandhi ministered patiently to victims and their families. Serving as his interpreter and aide, the anthropologist Nirmal Kumar Bose thought that Gandhi's 'tenderness' towards sufferers 'soothed them and lifted them above their sorrows'.

Yet this Noakhali Gandhi was also frank about the Hindu practice of untouchability and the need for caste Hindu repentance.

Noticing that East Bengal's 'untouchables', the Namashudras as they were called, had been braver than caste Hindus in responding to attacks, Gandhi insisted that village peace committees of Muslim and Hindu residents should include Namashudras; and he warned caste Hindu women that if they continued to disown the 'untouchables', more sorrow was in store. To Hindu women, he proposed a radical step on 3 January 1947 (in Chandipur):

> Invite a Harijan every day to dine with you. Or at least ask the
> Harijan to touch the food or the water before you consume
> it. Do penance for your sins.

Those aware of the India of 1947, even those aware of the India of
2017, know what a bold suggestion this was.

Recalling what Penderel Moon and Lord Wavell had said, it may
be asked: wasn't fighting untouchability also a political goal? Gandhi
indeed argued, right from 1916, that if high-caste Hindus did not
alter their treatment of low castes and 'untouchables', they would
neither deserve nor get independence. Yet for him the fight against
untouchability was above all a requirement of simple humanity.

When in June 1947 an unhappy Gandhi acquiesced in the
Partition to which leaders of the Indian National Congress had agreed
as the price for Indian independence, he reminded the Congress
of the time, where high-caste Hindus formed a large majority, that
independence, or the departure of the British, was only a step towards
goals that were as big or bigger.

'What about the "untouchables"?' he asked the All India Congress
Committee (AICC).

> If you say that 'untouchables' are nothing, the Adivasis are
> nothing, then you are not going to survive yourselves. But
> if you do away with the distinction of savarna and avarna,
> if you treat the Shudras, the 'untouchables' and the Adivasis
> as equals, then something good will have come out of a bad
> thing [the Partition].

Talented colleagues, men who would lead the future government
of free India, also spoke at this crucial AICC meeting, including
Jawaharlal Nehru, Vallabhbhai Patel, Abul Kalam Azad and Govind
Ballabh Pant. But Gandhi was the only one there to address the
question of the 'untouchables'.

His speech of less than ten minutes was more forward-looking than the utterances of younger colleagues. It underlined two other challenges that a free, if truncated, India would immediately face: Hindu–Muslim relations and the question of the princely states. Said Gandhi:

> In the three-quarters of the country that has fallen to our share, Hinduism is going to be tested. If you show the generosity of true Hinduism, you will pass in the eyes of the world. If not, you will have proved Mr. Jinnah's thesis that Muslims and Hindus are two separate nations...
>
> [T]hat some [princely] States should [want to] secede from India...is a very serious thing... [The princes] must recognize the paramountcy of the people as they recognized the paramountcy of the British Government...

■

Gandhi's passion against the shame of caste hierarchy and untouchability had a connection to 'Vaishnava Jana', that song about knowing the other person's pain. There were other texts too for nurturing that passion, scriptural and non-scriptural, Indian and non-Indian, and ugly realities always summoned it. But we should not underestimate the influence of 'Vaishnava Jana'.

That song was sung in Gandhi's large joint family when he was a child. His parents, older brothers, sister, half-sisters, cousins, uncles and aunts were all familiar with it; but *they* did not deduce the shame of untouchability from 'Vaishnava Jana'. People whose pain a good man should feel could not, in their view, include 'untouchables'.

When the boy Mohan was 'hardly yet twelve', his mother Putlibai told him that he was not to touch Uka, the 'untouchable' boy who cleaned the lavatory in the Gandhi house in Rajkot. Apparently Mohan had 'tussles' with her on the question and he questioned her reasoning, yet he tried to obey the injunction, which was that any accidental contact with Uka or any other 'untouchable' called for a cleansing bath.

If a bath could not be easily had, Mohan was to cancel the 'unholy touch', his mother told him, by touching any Muslim passing by. The second pollution would remove the first.

The boy taught by a loving mother, to whom he was deeply devoted, to view a section of Hindus and all Muslims as unclean and inferior by birth ended up fighting harder than anyone else against untouchability and for Hindu-Muslim partnership.

Despite considerable progress, caste justice remains distant today in India. Hindu-Muslim partnership too was only partially achieved. Independence was accompanied not only by Partition but also by great carnage, despite Gandhi's attempts to avert those outcomes. Later we will look at some of those attempts.

Here, let us merely note that after Pakistanis heard on the evening of 30 January 1948 that Gandhi had been killed, many of them skipped their meal that night. One of their tallest leaders, Mian Iftikharuddin of Lahore, referred to the preceding carnage against Hindu and Sikhs in Pakistan's West Punjab province and against Muslims in India's East Punjab province, and said:

> Each one of us who has raised his hand against innocent men, women and children during the past months, who has publicly or secretly entertained sympathy for such acts, is a collaborator in the murder of Mahatma Gandhi.

Eleven years later, in 1959, a thirty-year-old man called Martin Luther King, Jr., preaching in a church in Montgomery, Alabama, talked of Gandhi:

> They killed him, this man who had galvanized 400 million [Indians] for independence... One of his own fellow Hindus felt that he was a little too favourable toward the Moslems...

King was implying that independence was not Gandhi's sole or dominant goal. As he saw it, Gandhi was asking his people to feel the other person's pain.

■

Gandhi did not invent the words, addressed to the Almighty, 'Ishwar Allah Tero Naam (You are Ishwar, You are Allah)', but his life, message, and legacy are fused with it. When I visited Noakhali in November 2000, fifty-four years after Gandhi's trek there, I asked residents I bumped into on country roads if they remembered Gandhi. They did not know that I was Gandhi's grandson or someone from India.

The reply of a man who gave his name as Sirajul Islam Majumdar of village Kamalpur, a man who seemed to be in his late fifties and was the son, as he told me, of Dr Khaleelur Rahman Majumdar, was as follows:

> My father told us of 'Raghupati Raghav Raja Ram, Ishwar Allah Tero Naam'.

Sirajul Islam did not just pronounce the words. He sang them! This was fifty-four years after his father had heard them from Gandhi, and in immediate response to a question from one he was encountering by accident. Sirajul Islam then added with some pride, 'My grandfather protected Hindus on his roof during the rioting.'

As far as I know, the line 'Ishwar Allah Tero Naam' was not recited around the boy Mohan in his boyhood home in Rajkot. Gandhi seems to have first heard it only a year before his death. On 22 January 1947, when he had reached Paniala village in Noakhali, his grand-niece Manu sang the line at the daily multifaith prayer meeting, open to anyone interested, which had become part of Gandhi's life.

Observing that Paniala's Muslims, who had gathered in huge numbers, liked the verse, Gandhi asked Manu to sing the line 'daily from now on'. 'God Himself breathed it into your mind,' he told Manu.

The line has now been breathed into the minds of hundreds of millions in India, Pakistan and Bangladesh who see it as both a core Gandhi message and an obvious truth. Though called by various names, God was one.

And though Gandhi first heard the song only a year before his death, he believed in its truth from boyhood, if not from childhood. Here are some of Gandhi's recollections, offered at different times in his life. In 1942 he said:

> I believed even at [a] tender age that...it did not matter if I made no special effort to cultivate friendship with Hindus, but I must make friends with at least a few Muslims.

In 1947, Gandhi again claimed that his belief in 'complete brotherhood' among Hindus, Muslims and Parsis dated back to 'before 1885'—to 'before the Congress was born', he pointed out. 'At the time that communal unity possessed me, I was a lad twelve years old,' he added.

In January 1948, at the start of what would prove to be his last fast for Hindu-Muslim reconciliation, Gandhi again recalled his boyhood 'dream' of 'amity' between Hindus, Muslims and Parsis, dating that dream to Rajkot and to a time when he 'never even read the newspapers, could read English with difficulty, and my Gujarati was not satisfactory'.

In a talk given twenty years earlier, in 1927, Gandhi clearly recalled, without naming him, his Muslim friend from school, Mehtab, who also features, again without being named, in Gandhi's autobiography, which was written in the late 1920s.

In this 1927 talk Gandhi spoke of his 'vivid recollection [from his school years] of boys who put on an air because they had athletic skill and physical power'. But, said Gandhi, 'their pride went before destruction, because weaker ones, realizing their haughtiness, segregated them...and so they really dug their own graves'.

Gandhi had befriended the athletic, daring and self-isolated Mehtab, a classmate of Gandhi's brother Karsan, older than Mohandas by three years. This interesting Mohandas-Mehtab relationship continued when in 1897 or 1898 Mehtab joined Gandhi in South Africa as manager of the large house that Gandhi, by now a successful lawyer, kept in Durban.

The dramatic story of how that relationship in Durban ended within months is told in the autobiography. However, fourteen or fifteen years later, Mehtab's wife, Fatima, played a significant role, along with her mother, in the major Gandhi-led satyagraha of 1913 for the rights of Indian women and men in South Africa.

After his school years in Rajkot, and before his legal work in South Africa, Gandhi had spent three years, from 1888 to 1891, in London as a law student. There he learnt something about the prophet of Islam from Thomas Carlyle's *Heroes and Hero-Worship*, which an unnamed friend had recommended.

Interestingly, too, young Gandhi participated in meetings in London of the Anjuman-e-Islam, founded in 1886 for Muslim students by an Indian barrister, Abdullah Sohrawardy. We know the name of at least one Muslim student he befriended in London: Mazharul Haq from Bihar, a future president of the Muslim League. And we know that in London Gandhi noticed that some Muslim students were attracted by ideas of Pan-Islamism.

But the point to return to is this: the thought if not the precise words of 'Ishwar Allah Tero Naam' had germinated in Gandhi from his boyhood and youth.

■

In different corners of India, from posters stuck to a tree trunk maybe, or to a lamp post, wall, or billboard, a Gandhi wearing spectacles under a bald head often looks at Indians, usually next to a text which may read, 'Let us Make India Clean,' or a call of that sort.

For me, the eye-glasses are a reminder of Gandhi the reader, writer and independent thinker. For forty-five continuous years from 1903, when *Indian Opinion* first appeared in South Africa, to his death in 1948, Gandhi wrote for his journals. He wrote two books, *Satyagraha in South Africa* and his autobiography. And he wrote a phenomenal number of letters, using the left hand when his right was worn out.

Many letters were political, including some designed to prod or confront India's British rulers, but most were personal, dealing with specific issues raised by the addressee.

What I also take from Gandhi's probing spectacles is his repeated insistence that religious verses 'cannot be above reason and morality'.

In November 1917, when defenders of untouchability cited ancient verses to justify their practices, Gandhi replied:

> It is no good quoting verses from *Manusmriti* and other scriptures in defence... A number of verses in these scriptures are apocryphal, a number of them are quite meaningless...

Added Gandhi: 'Even slavery [in America] is not worse than [our untouchability]'.

In a preface in 1918 to a collection of poems on how 'untouchables' were being treated in Gujarat, Gandhi wrote, 'Shri Padhiar has given a heart-rending picture which cannot but fill the reader with horror to the very roots of his being,' and added that the poems should be 'read out to men and women in their millions the same way that [stories of Krishna in] the Bhagavat are read out...in every square'.

His spectacles should remind us of this Gandhi who not only championed reason but who a hundred years ago wanted India's millions to be made aware of the horrid realities of an evil practice.

■

With his ubiquitous pocket watch, Gandhi introduced punctuality to a nation that comprehended notions of infinity and eternity but seemed less committed to dates, hour and minutes. I also see the pocket watch, which was a symbol against wasting time (Gandhi called it theft), as a prod towards efficiency.

Among other things, Gandhi's watch reminds me that one of his innovations was to turn an unwieldy body called the Indian National Congress that gathered once a year into a fighting machine with elected committees at every level, from village or town to taluka, district and province, culminating in an All India Congress Committee and a year-round Working Committee that could assemble at short notice.

Asked in 1919 to design a new structure for the Congress, Gandhi not only produced a scheme; by 1920 his design was implemented.

As for the broom, sanitation was not only one of Gandhi's lifelong passions; it was constantly demonstrated in his ashrams and also at the great political and social gatherings that he, his colleagues and lieutenants organized.

Picking up a broom, Gandhi would start cleaning the mess that delegates, including distinguished ones, usually left at the venues of such gatherings. Some embarrassed fellow-participants would follow him in the exercise, but even the many who did not would remember that British rule was not the only ugly sight in India.

And at a time when some of India's finest minds sought to replicate in their land the West's crowded factory towns, Gandhi insisted that clean air and clean water were greater priorities. Thus on 6 January 1947 he told peasants in Chandipur in East Bengal that nothing was more important than

> how to get pure water in the villages, how to keep ourselves clean, how best to utilize the soil from which we have sprung, how to breathe in life's energy from the infinite sky above our head, how to draw fresh life from our surroundings and how best to use the sun's rays.

∎

The broom, the pocket watch and spectacles have *become* Gandhi logos, but the spinning wheel was his symbol by design. Again and again Gandhi said that the charkha was what he stood for.

By spinning on a small inexpensive wheel at home, any old man or woman, a youngster, the malnourished, the landless labourer, the unemployed, or the underemployed could make precious coppers and gain dignity.

The spinning wheel empowered the weak. It empowered the individual. It turned a consumer into a producer. It equalized the 'untouchable' with the Brahmin, demolished every caste barrier, taught elite, rich, and privileged Indians to earn their bread by the sweat of their brow.

Town dwellers or the better-off built a bond with spinners and weavers when they bought khadi or khaddar, cloth made from start to finish by hand.

The cloth the wheel made could be touched, felt, seen and displayed. By wearing khadi or khaddar, fighters for independence carried on their bodies a common, visible and proud flag of self-reliance.

Every man or woman who wore khadi, or carded, spun, or wove for it, felt tied by its threads to Mahatma Gandhi, to India's poor, to Swaraj, to satyagraha. The Arab poet, Mikhail Noema, wrote:

> The spindle in Gandhi's hand became sharper than the sword; the simple white sheet wrapping Gandhi's thin body was an armour-plate which guns from the fleets of the master of the seas could not pierce; and the goat of Gandhi became stronger than the British Lion.

■

To Gandhi, the spinning wheel also symbolized nonviolence. Here is what he said in 1938 in Bannu in the NWFP, then part of India and close to what became the Pakistan-Afghanistan border in 1947:

> The charkha is not my invention. It was there before... God whispered into my ear: 'If you want to work through nonviolence, you have to proceed with small things, not big'.

The young Gandhi had *not* been a votary of nonviolence. When he was a schoolboy in the 1880s, the violent 1857 Revolt, though centred in northern India, was a recent memory in Gujarat too. The boy Mohan welcomed talk of driving the British out by physical force, a task for which, so his friend Mehtab told him, boys needed to strengthen themselves by eating meat.

But that generation of young Indians was also attracted by social reforms inspired by the British advent, including notions that children should not marry (Mohan and Kastur, better known as Kasturba, were both twelve when they were married) and that widows should be permitted to remarry.

In a talk that eighteen-year-old Mohan gave to his school before leaving for London—he was the first youth in Kathiawar from his Bania caste to go to England—he said he would work for 'big reforms' and hoped that others would too.

In his three years in England, Mohandas did not run into hostility or superiority from the Britons he met. He loved his London years. A journal he kept on the ship that brought him back to India refers to 'dear London' and its charms.

But after he had returned to India, the rough behaviour towards him of the chief imperial agent in Rajkot, Charles Ollivant, who ordered Mohandas thrown out of his imperial office, shocked him, the more so because Mohandas had met Ollivant in London, when the officer was on leave, and had found him friendly enough.

Recovering from this shock, in May 1893 Gandhi went to South Africa to assist with a law suit that a rich Muslim trader and shipowner known to Gandhi's family, and belonging like the Gandhis to Kathiawar, had launched against a cousin.

Within days of arriving in South Africa, Gandhi learnt lessons about racism, including when he was summarily ejected at Pietermaritzburg station in the British colony of Natal from the first-class coach for which he held a proper ticket.

Believing that London would chastise Natal, Gandhi placed hopes in imperialism. Victoria, Empress of India and Queen of England, who had promised equality between races after the 1857 Revolt, was still on the throne. Gandhi sang 'God Save the Queen' with gusto and taught his family to do likewise.

In the end, however, it was satyagraha, or nonviolent resistance, rather than imperialism that brought valuable gains to Indians in South Africa. How Gandhi found satyagraha in South Africa will be discussed in the next chapter. Here, let us mark that despite disappointments the Gandhi returning to India in 1915 remained a believer in Empire.

In March 1918, this is what he privately said to a talented new colleague and secretary, Mahadev Desai:

> I have to cruelly suppress my urges. Ever since I read the history of the East India Company, my mind refuses to be loyal to the British Empire and I have to make a strenuous effort to stem the tide of rebellion. The first thought that rises up in the mind is that the British should be driven out of India bag and baggage. But a feeling deep down in me persists that India's good lies in [the] British connection, and so I force myself to love them.

He would summon the will to love the British, but in 1920 he decided that he would also fight the Empire. In Chapter 4 we will look in detail at the Gandhi-Empire clash. Here, we may merely mark that in 1930, the year of the Salt March, he told a colleague, Kaka Kalelkar, 'I was born to destroy this evil government.'

Two years later, he said again to Kalelkar: 'Just as a pregnant woman takes care of her health for the sake of the baby in her womb, I take care of myself for the sake of the Swaraj that is supposed to be in my womb'.

In between, in 1931, he told William Shirer, American reporter and future author of *The Rise and Fall of the Third Reich*, 'You will see, my dear Mr Shirer! We shall gain our freedom in my lifetime.'

Yet in March 1930, while announcing to the viceroy, Lord Irwin, his intention to launch a campaign of disobedience, this very Gandhi had added: 'If I have equal love for your people with mine, it will not long remain hidden'.

Whether or not the Empire's guardians recognized Gandhi's love for the British, they understood the strength of his nonviolent lathi. Here are three imperial verdicts.

On the Non-Cooperation Movement of 1920-22. 'Gandhi's was the most colossal experiment in world history, and it came within an inch of succeeding': Lord George Lloyd, Governor of Bombay, 1918-23.

On the Salt March and related satyagrahas of 1930. 'Such humiliation and defiance...has not been known since the British first trod the soil of India': Winston Churchill in the House of Commons, 12 March 1931.

On Quit India, August 1942. 'By far the most serious rebellion since that of 1857': Lord Linlithgow, viceroy, in a letter dated 31 August 1942 to Prime Minister Churchill.

■

In the final weeks of British rule, other leaders of India's independence movement softened their language towards the Empire, but Gandhi remained vigilant about India's dignity. The love he wished to harbour was of an equal.

This came across when at the end of June 1947 the viceroy, Lord Mountbatten, evidently told Gandhi that 'if Congress members' of the viceroy's interim executive 'did not adopt a helpful attitude' the British might not quit on 15 August, by then the agreed date of independence. It seems that Mountbatten added that 'if partition had not been [agreed to] during British occupation, the Hindus being the majority party would have never allowed partition and held the Muslims by force under subjection'.

In a letter of protest, Gandhi informed Mountbatten that his remarks had 'startled' him.

Reminding the forty-seven-year-old viceroy, who was also a famed admiral, that the Congress had 'solemnly declared' that it would not 'hold by force' any Muslim-majority area that might wish to separate, the seventy-seven-year-old Gandhi added:

> Even if I stand alone, I swear by nonviolence and truth, together standing for the highest order of courage, before which the atom bomb pales into significance, what to say of a fleet of Dreadnoughts.

After this reminder from Gandhi that the independence agreed upon was not a favour from the Empire, thoughts of postponing the date were abandoned.

■

Although Hindu-Muslim violence was marring the coming of independence, Gandhi shared the pride being felt across the subcontinent. On 10 June, he said in a letter to a friend:

> For sixty years we have been in the thick of the fight, and now we have ushered the goddess of liberty into our courtyard.

Other Indians felt similarly. However, what Gandhi said in April 1947 to leaders from Asia who had gathered in New Delhi at Nehru's initiative could not have come from anyone else:

> *1 April*: All the Asian representatives have come together. Is it in order to wage a war against Europe, against America or against non-Asiatics? I say most emphatically 'No'. This is not India's mission.
>
> *2 April*: The first of [Asia's] wise men was Zoroaster. He belonged to the East. He was followed by the Buddha who belonged to the East—India. Who followed the Buddha? Jesus, who came from the East. Before Jesus was Moses who belonged to Palestine though he was born in Egypt. After Jesus came Mohammed… I do not know of a single person in the world to match these men of Asia. And then what happened? Christianity became disfigured when it went to the West.
>
> [T]he message of Asia…is not to be learnt through Western spectacles or by imitating the atom bomb. If you want to give a message to the West, it must be the message of love and the message of truth. I want you to go away with the thought that Asia has to conquer the West through love and truth.
>
> Of course, I believe in 'one world'. How can I possibly do otherwise, when I became an inheritor of the message of love that these great unconquerable teachers left for us?
>
> In this age of democracy, in this age of awakening of the poorest of the poor, you can redeliver this message with the greatest emphasis. You will complete the conquest of the West

not through vengeance because you have been exploited, but with real understanding...This conquest will be loved by the West itself.

■

Four days before freedom, the BBC asked for a message from the Empire's chief foe, who found himself in Calcutta at the time, hoping to proceed to Noakhali. The moment of triumph was also one of sadness over violent incidents, and an embarrassed Gandhi felt he had nothing to say to London. The BBC pleaded: his message would be broadcast in several languages, Gandhi was told it would reach the world. Through Nirmal Kumar Bose, Gandhi repeated his unwillingness:

I must not yield to the temptation. They must forget that I know English.

To help bring peace to Calcutta, which was seeing violence, Gandhi, accompanied by Huseyn Suhrawardy, seen by many of the city's Hindus as the architect of anti-Hindu violence, moved into Hydari Manzil, 'an old abandoned Muslim house' in Beliaghata, a run-down Hindu-majority locality where Muslim residents felt threatened, with some leaving Beliaghata.

Accusing Gandhi of a pro-Muslim bias, a band of angry young Hindus asked him to move out of Beliaghata. He had two sessions with the group, including one in Suhrawardy's presence. If Beliaghata's Hindus invited their Muslim neighbours to return, he said to them, he and Suhrawardy would move to a predominantly Muslim area until Hindus were invited to return there. The young men were 'completely won over' by this offer, and another irate group was pacified when Suhrawardy boldly admitted responsibility for the Great Calcutta Killings that had taken place a year earlier.

The next day, 14 August, was wonderfully different. Gandhi wrote about it himself in his journal, *Harijan*:

In their thousands [Calcutta's residents] began to embrace one another and...to pass freely through places...considered to be points of danger by one party or the other. Indeed, Hindus were taken to their masjids by their Muslim brethren and the latter were taken by their Hindu brethren to the mandirs. Both with one voice shouted 'Jai Hind' or 'Hindus-Muslims! Be one'.

India was independent before the next morning. Thus it was from a Muslim house in one of Calcutta's poorest corners that Gandhi greeted independence. He recited his pre-dawn prayers, plied his charkha, remembered Mahadev Desai, whose birthday it also was, and said fruit juice would be his only food during the day.

Though Gandhi had not felt like lighting lamps, fireworks had lit up Calcutta for all of the previous night. He wrote the day's quota of letters. One was addressed to his Quaker friend in England, Agatha Harrison:

My dear Agatha, This letter I am dictating whilst I am spinning. You know, my way of celebrating great events, such as today's, is to thank God for it and, therefore, to pray. This prayer must be accompanied by a fast, if the taking of fruit juices may be so described. And then as a mark of identification with the poor and dedication there must be [extra] spinning... My love to all our friends.

So on Independence Day the Empire's principal foe sent his love to British friends. In the afternoon he conducted a prayer meeting in an open ground in Beliaghata. Thousands of Muslims and Hindus attended. Gandhi felt that 'the joy of fraternization [was] leaping up from hour to hour'.

In a short prayer talk, Gandhi expressed joy at the turn of events in Calcutta and concern over the news coming in of 'madness' in Lahore and of flooding in the Chittagong area, now part of Pakistan. He ended the talk by asking Calcutta's residents to 'treat the Europeans who stayed in India with the same regard as they would expect for themselves'. He had heard that Europeans were being compelled to utter independence cries.

In the evening, making an unusual request, Gandhi asked to be driven anonymously around the city. He wanted to take in more of Calcutta's joy and also to probe, in his words, whether it was 'Miracle or Accident.' On the streets he heard, from the joint throats of Hindus and Muslims, the cry, 'Long Live Hindustan and Pakistan'.

Eid day fell—three short days after Independence—on 18 August. Half a million Hindus and Muslims attended Gandhi's prayer meeting, held on the grounds of Calcutta's Mohammedan Sporting Football Club. 'I will never be able to forget the scene I have witnessed today,' said Gandhi.

In the months that remained before his death, Gandhi and India would witness other memorable scenes, including those of great pain and sorrow, but we have seen that Gandhi's thirst for friendship and dignity among human beings was not weaker than his love for India's liberty.

CHAPTER 3

GANDHI'S GIFT AND HIS GOD

A couple of questions are asked in this chapter. How did Gandhi hit upon satyagraha or nonviolent resistance, which was his gift to the world? Secondly, who or what was Gandhi's God?

As the psychoanalyst Erik Erikson put it, the boy Mohan, greatly loved by both father and mother, possessed a 'precocious conscience'. For instance, in about the middle of 1885, when help was needed by Karsandas (Karamchand or 'Kaba', Gandhi's second son), who had piled up a debt of twenty-five rupees, younger brother Mohan, now close to sixteen, clipped a bit of the solid gold from what Karsan wore as an armlet, and the debt was cleared.

At this point Mohan and Karsan were carrying another guilt in their bosoms: their secret eating of meat, which had been prodded by Mehtab's taunts and arguments. The change in the armlet was noticed by the women in the family, who spoke about it, and Mohan decided he would confess his theft.

Prudence was at work along with Mohan's conscience: it was wiser, and also more honourable, to come clean before questions were asked. Probably Mohan also wanted to protect Karsan, who was increasingly seen as the black sheep of the family.

We should recognize that Mohan did not wish to admit his and Karsan's meat-eating, which Mohan had abandoned for the time being, telling himself he would resume it after his parents were no more.

Mohan did not dare to *speak* of his theft to his father, the former diwan of Porbandar, Rajkot and Wankaner. He wrote out a confession and handed it to a sick Kaba Gandhi who was lying on his back on a plain wooden bed in the courtyard of the Gandhis' Rajkot home.

The confession said his father would now know that his much-loved son was merely a common thief. But the son would steal no more and was asking for forgiveness and also for adequate punishment. The note closed with a request that the father should not punish himself. Here are the well-known words from the autobiography:

> I was trembling as I handed the confession... He read it through, and pearl-drops trickled down his cheeks, wetting the paper. For a moment he closed his eyes in thought and then tore up the note. He had sat up to read it. He again lay down. I also cried. I could see my father's agony. If I were a painter, I could draw a picture of the whole scene today. Those pearl-drops of love cleansed my heart and washed my sin away.

It was a brave deed, and yet (as Erikson points out) the Mohan of this confession seems to be in control. Any anxiety in his mind relates to what might happen to his father, not to him.

Very few spaces, and very few incidents, in a joint family like that of the Gandhis were private. Certainly Mohan's unusual confession was not. Everyone knew of it, and everyone remembered it.

Including Gandhi's older sister Raliat, who was in her nineties when she died and had survived her brother. Raliat never fully forgave the brother's departures from tradition. But in old age she recalled her brother's boyhood confession to Gandhi's biographer, Pyarelal.

■

Gandhi would always claim that his moral journey and political quest were one and the same; that the latter flowed from the former; and that he fought for independence, for Hindu-Muslim partnership and for the ending of high and low because his conscience demanded these goals.

There were times of tension between the two drives, yet the

morally driven Gandhi is a real person, called to be a slave to a force which at different times he calls conscience, or the inner voice, or God.

Gandhi is a foe of human domination but he craves God's domination. He rises against tyranny but wants to fall on his knees before his conscience or God. Both impulses can be seen at the start of his life, throughout his life, and at the end of his life.

∎

The moral and the political came together for Gandhi in South Africa in 1906, when in the hilly terrain of Zululand he obtained his first clear insight into the potential of nonviolent struggle, or what he would call satyagraha, or 'clinging to the truth'.

Before relating that story let me mention a notable weakness in South Africa's Gandhi. He not only confined himself, for much of the time, to the Indian cause, he also entertained, especially in his early years in South Africa, and in common with the rest of the Indian community there, some stereotypical and derogatory views about Africans, though on occasion he went dramatically and inspiringly beyond his Indian 'tent'.

The struggles of South Africa's Blacks and Indians tended to remain separate, if also mutually reinforcing, while Gandhi was there over a hundred years ago.

After a Zulu chief rejected a new British tax in 1906, a white man sent to collect the tax was speared to death; another white man was also killed. In punishment, twelve Zulus were blown to death at the mouth of a cannon before an audience that included several chiefs. The Zulu revolt persisted, and military action to crush it was announced.

In his journal *Indian Opinion*, Gandhi wrote in April 1906 of 'important events, the effects of which will not be forgotten for many years' and of 'great changes likely to take place in South Africa'. 'The Indians and other Blacks,' he added, 'have much to ponder and act with circumspection'.

Though he doubted the revolt's wisdom, Gandhi's sympathy was with the Zulus, 'who (Gandhi noted) had harmed no Indian'. But South Africa's Indian community existed on British sufferance, and Gandhi and his associates felt they had to support the authorities. In *Indian Opinion* Gandhi wrote:

> What is our duty in these calamitous times in the colony? It is not for us to say whether the revolt…is justified or not. We are in Natal by virtue of the British power. Our very existence depends upon it. It is therefore our duty to render whatever help we can.

To the governor of Natal, Gandhi offered, with (as he put it) 'the community's permission', an Indian Ambulance Corps. The governor accepted the Indian offer, and Gandhi found himself leading a twenty-strong corps of twelve South Indians, five Gujaratis, two from Punjab and one from Calcutta. Of the twenty, fourteen were Hindus and six Muslims.

So a Gandhi who wants equal rights for Indians takes an Indian Ambulance Corps to support British troops who are suppressing a revolt by Natal's native Zulus.

If this sounds shocking, we should note that John Dube, the Zulu leader (and Gandhi's friend) who would help found the African National Congress, said, also in 1906, that while the Zulus had serious grievances, 'at a time like this we should all refrain from discussing them, and assist the government to suppress the rebellion'.

For four weeks in June–July 1906, the Indian Ambulance Corps served in Mapumulo, Umvoti Valley and Imati Valley in the Zulu country, carrying on stretchers Zulu 'friendlies' mistakenly shot by British soldiers, or nursing Zulu friendlies and Zulu suspects wounded by British lashes.

In addition, Gandhi compounded and dispensed prescriptions for wounded or sick white soldiers: he had learnt these skills earlier in Durban. Finding that the military exercise he was supporting was above all a manhunt, and hearing 'rifles exploding' (as he would put it) 'like crackers in innocent hamlets', Gandhi was assailed by qualms. His conscience was somewhat eased by the fact that he and his corps nursed innocent Zulus who would otherwise have been uncared for. The British doctor in charge of ambulance had told Gandhi that white nurses were unwilling to attend to wounded Zulus.

With or without the wounded, Gandhi and his colleagues marched long distances, at times forty miles a day. Gandhi tells us that in his treks 'through these solemn solitudes' he 'often fell into deep thought'.

Erikson concludes that the exercises of cleansing the gunshot wounds and binding rents made by the lash aroused in Gandhi 'both a deeper identification with the maltreated and a stronger aversion against all forms of male sadism'.

Also, and this Erikson does not mention, Gandhi was reminded of India's 1857 rebellion, which had witnessed violence from the Indian side and brutality from the British, who flogged sympathizers of rebels, blew men off the mouths of cannons, and suppressed the revolt. In 1893-94 in South Africa, before his hours were swallowed by legal and community work, Gandhi had studied six volumes by John Kaye and Colonel George Malleson on the 1857 Revolt and absorbed the fact that the Revolt had consolidated British power in India, even as the Zulu revolt seemed to be doing in South Africa.

In Zululand, Gandhi saw fresh proof of that lesson. Being excited into violence against the strong in arms was folly.

This was of immediate relevance for South Africa's Indian community. At this precise time, Indians living in South Africa's Transvaal region, with whom Gandhi was in close contact, were agitated about new laws threatening their residence there. If a struggle was required in the Transvaal, which comprised another part of South Africa, what form should it take?

Gandhi concluded that any Indian struggle would have to be nonviolent. Also, he reached decisions on personal questions on which he had been reflecting for some time. One was that he should possess the strength and flexibility of the celibate, or the brahmachari.

Indian tradition honoured such a person, and in Gandhi's view so did Christianity. He thought that celibacy would make him more effective in future struggles.

Secondly, he should free himself from the drag of possessions. By now Gandhi and his wife Kastur had four sons. Henceforth he would not live for wealth, or sex, or for expanding his family. The less he had the more he would become.

He also sensed a wider role for himself. He would say afterwards: 'A mission…came to me in 1906, namely, to spread truth and nonviolence among mankind in the place of violence and falsehood in all walks of life.'

He had found a new purpose for his life: demonstrating satyagraha to the world. His weapon for realizing the goal of Indian independence, satyagraha, would also foster Hindu–Muslim friendship and the ending of high and low. It would integrate Gandhi's passions.

And whereas many others in India also aimed at independence, or Hindu–Muslim friendship, or social equality, though seldom with Gandhi's intensity, satyagraha was his unique gift to India and the world.

'My people were excited,' Gandhi would recall in 1931, referring to the year 1906 and the crisis before the Transvaal Indians, 'and there was talk of wreaking vengeance. I had then to choose between allying myself to violence or finding out some other method of meeting the crisis…and it came to me that we should refuse to obey legislation that was degrading and let them put us in jail if they liked'

Two months after his Zulu treks ended, the Transvaal Indians, led by Gandhi, launched their first nonviolent defiance or, as it would soon be called, satyagraha, with Gandhi saying on 11 September 1906—we should mark the date, 11 September—'I can boldly declare, and with certainty, that so long as there are even a handful of men true to their pledge, there can be only one end to the struggle, and that is victory'.

Thus a battlefield exercise conducted with an uneasy conscience became a laboratory and a springboard for Gandhi.

Holding that 'the turning point in Gandhi's personal life came in 1906' in Zululand, the anti-nuclear weapons campaigner Jonathan Schell reminds us that whereas in both East and West, holy vows have usually been accompanied by withdrawal from the world and from politics, 'Gandhi proceeded in exactly the opposite direction'. His vows had freed him not from but *for* action.

■

Let us try to understand the thinking of the man behind satyagraha.

Hindu tradition held that renouncers obtain power, and Gandhi claimed to see that truth also in the Cross. For the Indian people, Gandhi's appeal was certainly enhanced by his simple lifestyle, his vows, his fasts, his barefoot walks and his refusal to give or seek special treatment to members of his family.

At times his eldest son Harilal charged that goaded by personal ambition the father sacrificed his sons, and in September 1901, five years *before* the Zululand experience, there was a significant exchange in Durban between a Gandhi a month short of his thirty-second birthday and his wife Kastur, who was a few months older than him.

After several years in Durban, the couple, their four sons (Harilal, thirteen, Manilal, nine, Ramdas, three, and Devadas, one) and a thirteen-year-old nephew, Gokul, the son of his sister Raliat, who had been widowed, were returning to India, so they thought, for good. (The assumption was wrong. Summoned by the community, Gandhi would in fact return to South Africa in 1902, and his family would follow him back.)

As a lawyer and community leader, the Gandhi about to leave Durban in 1901 had done a good deal for Natal's Indians. To show appreciation, the community and clients had given costly presents: a gold necklace for Kastur, other gold chains, gold watches and diamond rings. Most gifts were from the community, some from clients.

After an evening when many gifts were given, an agitated Gandhi spent a sleepless night. Should a public servant accept gifts? Since his clients too were helpers in public work, should he take what *they* had given? Later Gandhi truthfully recalled: 'It was difficult for me to forego gifts worth hundreds (of pounds).'

But he found it more difficult to keep the gifts. That night he drafted a letter placing the presents in a trust for the community. In the morning he held a 'consultation' with Kastur, but only after securing the boys' agreement. Apparently, the three older boys, Harilal, Gokul and Manilal, not only told their father that they did not need the presents, they also agreed to persuade their mother.

This did not prove easy. Kastur fought with passion and logic both. The boys might dance to his tune, she told Gandhi, but 'what about my daughters-in-law?' The future was unknown, and she would be 'the last person to part with gifts so lovingly given'. She cried, too.

Gandhi said the boys would not marry young. When they did marry, their wives would be free from the lure of ornaments; if, however, ornaments were needed, Kastur could ask him.

'Ask you? I know you by this time. You deprived me of my ornaments... Fancy you offering to get ornaments for my daughters-in-law! You who are trying to make sadhus of my boys from today!'

Erikson's translation of the last remark is, 'You want them to be saints before they are men.' Saying, 'No, the ornaments will not be returned,' Kastur asked a proper legal question: 'And pray what right have you to my necklace?'

In a merciless response, Gandhi asked if the necklace was given for her service or his.

'I agree,' Kastur said. 'But,' she added, 'service rendered by you is as good as rendered by me. I have toiled and moiled for you day and night. Is that no service? You force all and sundry on me, making me weep bitter tears, and I slaved for them.'

'These were pointed thrusts, and some of them went home,' Gandhi would later acknowledge. But his mind was made up. In his own words, he 'somehow succeeded in extorting' her consent. The gifts were all returned.

If we feel that the 1901 'consultation' was loaded in his favour, and that the boys had been unfairly enlisted by the father, it is good also to recognize that we know of this conversation only because Gandhi related it, which he did because he was uneasy about the pressure he had applied.

Given the size of his goals, a tension in Gandhi's life was inescapable. In 1924, after writing in his journal *Young India* of 'my own dearest relatives', Gandhi added: 'Sometimes love's anguish left deep scars on the loved ones, but it left much deeper ones on the lover's bosom'.

When, in January 1928, the Gandhis' third son, Ramdas, married Nirmala Vora at the Sabarmati Ashram, a wedding arranged by the parents, the Gandhis' gifts to the couple were a copy of the Gita, a book of prayer songs, a 'takli' or spindle for spinning, and two rosaries made of thread spun by Gandhi.

Speaking after a short religious ceremony, Gandhi choked while acknowledging the poverty he had imposed on his sons. Ramdas was asked to be the bride's 'true friend' and 'not her master'. 'You will both earn your bread by the sweat of your brow as poor people do… Let the Gita be to you a mine of diamonds.'

Most of the time, there was no one with whom Gandhi could talk of *his* heartaches. Not, for instance, when as a twenty-two-year-old in 1891 he heard on landing in India from London that the mother he was 'pining to see' had died. 'Most of my cherished hopes were shattered,' he would write more than thirty years later.

Not when Rasik, a much loved seventeen-year-old grandson, died in 1929, though Gandhi, who had helped raise Rasik, son of Gandhi's oldest son, Harilal, wrote a piece on Rasik that he headlined, 'Sunset in the Morning'.

This bearer of India's hopes, this searcher after truth, who was always on the give, consoling and giving courage, almost never received the reassuring words, 'I understand you', or 'I feel for you', or 'I love you'. In his moments of trial, only God solaced him. Or his conscience, or an inner spirit.

In 1935, Harilal's indiscretions produced unhappy headlines. Kasturba wrote to the son:

> Your father does not speak anything about this before anybody.
> But the shock...breaks his heart to pieces.

The most humanly dramatic lines in Gandhi's life—whether of heartbreak or accomplishment, grief or ecstasy—were ones he could not utter. He seemed to have had no one to utter to. Once in a while, as we have seen, a solitary Gandhi would transmit his emotion via pen to paper, and share it with the world. More often, he vented it in silent communion with his Maker.

And he always bounced back.

We know of his unfulfilled desire in his early twenties, right after he returned from his London law studies, to be a writer. He was deflected from pursuing that desire by his confrontation with Charles Ollivant, which put him on the path to South Africa and a lifelong fight against domination.

More than four decades later, in the autumn of 1936, a sixty-seven-year-old Gandhi who had just started a new ashram in central India, far from his native Gujarat, was asked to preside at a gathering of Gujarati writers in Ahmedabad. Addressing the writers, he remembered his unfulfilled wish and came out with intriguing sentences:

> I have some interests which I cannot satisfy. A good many of these have become extinguished.... Anandshankarbhai told me that a poetry symposium was held here. I had wished to go to the lecture on the archaeological work in Indore. But I neither went to the lecture nor attended the poetry symposium...
>
> I have settled in a village [Segaon] which I did not go seeking, but which came to me. Likewise I had not gone around looking for satyagraha [i.e. satyagraha too 'came' to him].
>
> Many of the women from this village give their love to me much against my will. If however I were to accept their love, my vow of faithfulness to my wife would be put to shame. Hence I regard them as my mothers...
>
> When I went to South Africa, I took some Gujarati books

with me. Taylor's *Gujarati Grammar* was one of them. I like
it very much.

There was a time when a large number of women stayed
with me in South Africa. I had become father or brother to
women belonging to about sixty families. There were pretty
women as well as plain ones among them. Although these
women were illiterate, I brought out the courage in them and
they went to jail as bravely as men.

These remarks reveal a vulnerable, 'normal' Gandhi easy to relate
to as also the exceptional Gandhi because of whom women went
bravely to prison. The former has often remained hidden.

■

Most callers in the final fifteen years of his life thought that Gandhi
looked youthful rather than old, and also striking, despite his large
ears (like those of Mickey Mouse, a later generation would say) and
a similarly large nose that pointed downwards, with the lower lip
pushing up to meet the nose.

His laughter was specially noticed. He smiled, grinned, chuckled,
crackled, or laughed heartily, and usually those meeting him found
themselves laughing too. As Nehru said, Gandhi brought a breeze
to a room he entered.

Here is what William Shirer, the author of *The Rise and Fall
of the Third Reich,* said after one of several meetings he had with
Gandhi in the 1930s and 1940s:

In no time at all Gandhi had us all laughing and completely
at our ease... If in this world of varied personalities there is a
single man even half as charming as Gandhi, I have not seen him.

And he enjoyed others' jokes. Writing, in 1932, from a Pune prison
to a friend in southern India, Srinivasa Sastri, Gandhi said, 'Sardar
Vallabhbhai is with me. His jokes make me laugh until I can laugh
no more, not once but several times a day'.

Yet Gandhi's gaiety was matched by a discernible presence of sorrow. Nehru noticed 'deep pools of sadness' in Gandhi's twinkling eyes, and Hansa Mehta, one of the many talented women who joined Gandhi's movement after the Salt March, spoke for other sensitive observers too when she referred to a great pathos in Gandhi, adding, 'I always felt deeply moved in his presence.'

Some of the sadness undoubtedly came from the self-suppression we have looked at: he couldn't do what he had wanted to do. Then there was his eldest son, Harilal, who seldom stayed in one place or held down a job or looked after his children. Every reminder of Harilal's distress was a knife-stab for his parents.

A toll was taken, too, by Gandhi's inner conflicts, including over who at any given time were more 'his people' or 'family' than others, and over how hard or soft he should be with those close to him. Another layer of suppressed unhappiness may have been formed by a tension we will look at later in this chapter, between the voices, as he heard them, of universal truth and of India.

■

One person who recognized Gandhi's need for human warmth was Tagore's niece, Saraladevi Chaudhurani, who had involved herself in militant nationalism between 1903 and 1905. Three years younger than Gandhi, she had first met him in Calcutta at the end of 1901, but it was not until eighteen years later, when this Bengali lady was the wife of a prominent public figure in Lahore, that she grew close to Gandhi, who spent several months during 1919-1920 in Punjab.

Within days of his arrival in Lahore in October 1919, Gandhi would write to a close associate in Ahmedabad, Anasuya Sarabhai: 'Saraladevi's company is very endearing. She looks after me very well'.

The following months saw a special relationship between the two, with Gandhi overcoming an earlier caution he had expressed regarding exclusive relationships and briefly thinking of a 'spiritual marriage', as he thought of it, with Saraladevi.

We must conclude that Saraladevi conveyed to Gandhi an

aesthetic, political and possibly erotic appeal. She wrote, spoke and sang well. Politically, she represented a Tagore connection, the province of Bengal, and, from her past, the strand of patriotic violence. He may have imagined a merger with her helping him win all of India to nonviolent satyagraha.

Whether or not he consciously toyed with such considerations, they probably influenced him. But this unusual seven-month relationship ended in June 1920.

Gandhi's twenty-year-old son Devadas, his twenty-eight-year-old secretary Mahadev Desai, a nephew, Mathuradas Trikamdas (the grandson of his half-sister Muliben), and a close South Indian political associate, Chakravarti Rajagopalachari, who was nine years younger than Gandhi, had asked Gandhi to think of the consequences for Kasturba, for people like them, and for Gandhi himself if he continued the special relationship.

Rajagopalachari warned Gandhi that he was nursing 'a most dreadful delusion'. Before long Gandhi would start calling Rajagopalachari his conscience-keeper.

Thirteen years later, in 1933, Gandhi would say that he had been saved from 'rushing into hellfire' by the thought of Kasturba and because of interventions by Devadas, Desai and Mathuradas. In 1935, Gandhi told Margaret Sanger, after referring to Kasturba's illiteracy, that he had 'nearly slipped' after meeting 'a woman with a broad, cultural education' but had fortunately been freed from a 'trance'.

Shattered when Gandhi informed her that their relationship could not continue, Saraladevi complained that she had 'put in one pan all the joys and pleasures of the world, and in the other Bapu and his laws, and committed the folly of choosing the latter'. She demanded an explanation, which Gandhi finally tried to offer in a letter he sent in December 1920:

I have been analysing my love for you. I have reached a definition of spiritual [marriage]. It is a partnership between two persons of the opposite sex where the physical is wholly absent. It is therefore possible between brother and sister, father and daughter. It is possible only between two brahmacharis in thought, word and deed...

Have we that exquisite purity, that perfect coincidence, that perfect merging, that identity of ideals, the self-forgetfulness, that fixity of purpose, that trustfulness? For me I can answer plainly that it is only an aspiration. I am unworthy of that companionship with you... This is the big letter I promised. With dearest love I still subscribe myself, Your L.G.

The initials stood for Law Giver, the title with which she used to tease Gandhi. The letter could not of course assuage Saraladevi's feelings, but it is suggestive of the struggle inside Gandhi's heart. In the years that followed, Saraladevi criticized Gandhi, at times accusing him of allowing nonviolence to break out in hatred, at other times saying that he possessed a Christo-Buddhist rather than a Hindu frame of mind.

Communication did not cease, however. In the 1940s, at her instance, Gandhi suggested her son Dipak's name to Jawaharlal as a possible match for his daughter Indira. That idea did not work out, but after Saraladevi and Gandhi were both no more, Dipak married Radha, the daughter of Gandhi's nephew and close colleague, Maganlal Gandhi. Saraladevi and Gandhi had known of this romance. She passed away in 1945; her husband had died in 1923.

■

Who or what was Gandhi's God? What was his religion?

The joint family in which Mohandas was raised was loyal to the Vaishnava tradition the family and other Modh Banias had inherited, which called for ceremonies at temples of Rama and Krishna, and the older Gandhi would often refer to the Ramayana story, which was frequently recited in his boyhood home.

More liberal than others from his Vaishnavite jaati, Gandhi's parents also worshipped at the 'rival' Shiva temple, and their home was often visited by Jain monks. At times Muslim and Zoroastrian friends visited Kaba Gandhi in his home and talked about their faiths, but the boy Mohan harboured a bias against Christianity. He had felt offended, he informs us in the autobiography, when in his hearing a European preacher slighted Hindu gods at 'a corner near the high school'.

Equally, the creation story in an ancient Hindu text, the *Manusmriti*, which the boy Mohan found among his father's religious books, not only 'did not impress him very much', it made him 'incline somewhat towards atheism', a position strengthened by Mohan's daydreams, in the company of Karsan and Mehtab, of driving out the British.

The three London years removed the atheism and the bias against Christianity; it also taught young Gandhi the truths of the Gita and also of Buddhism. In London, he read Edwin Arnold's *The Song Celestial*, a translation of the Bhagavad Gita. Curiously enough, he had not come across the Gita in Rajkot. He also read, in London, Arnold's *Light of Asia*, which told the Buddha story.

For the rest of his life, Gandhi spoke of *The Song Celestial* as the best English translation of the Gita, which would become an inseparable part of his life, and on which he wrote a significant commentary himself in the 1920s.

His London years also gave to Gandhi a lifelong interest in Christianity which, to begin with, brought him close to a conversion.

In London, he heard famous preachers including Charles Spurgeon, the Congregationalist Joseph Parker, and Frederic William Farrar, who would become dean of Canterbury. He read the Bible and was bowled over by the Sermon on the Mount.

In his first year in South Africa, Gandhi went down on his knees many times along with Christian friends who prayed for him, and he journeyed to attend a great Christian convention in Wellington, forty miles from Cape Town.

In the end, Gandhi decided that he would accept metaphorically but not literally that by his death Jesus had redeemed the sins of the world, and he could not see Jesus as the only incarnate son of God.

Leo Tolstoy's *The Kingdom of God is Within You*, which he read in South Africa in 1894, 'overwhelmed' Gandhi (he would say in the autobiography) and the five commandments underlined by Tolstoy from the Sermon on the Mount—do not hate, do not lust, do not hoard, do not kill, love your enemies—went directly to Gandhi's heart.

In a talk in Ahmedabad in 1928, Gandhi recalled the impact Tolstoy's book had made on him:

> When I went to England, I was a votary of violence, I had faith in it and none in non-violence. After I read [Tolstoy's] book, that lack of faith in non-violence vanished.

Also in South Africa, the businessman who had hired him, Abdullah Sheth, asked Gandhi to study Islam. Gandhi read George Sale's translation of the Quran and other Islamic books. Unconvinced that he should embrace Christianity or Islam, and not certain either that Hinduism with its untouchability and 'a multitude of sects and castes' was a perfect religion, Gandhi remembered a key thought from Jainism, which was that doubt should accompany every certainty.

To his friend in India, Rajchandra, a Jain who was a poet, a jeweller, and a scholar of Jainism and Hinduism, Gandhi sent twenty-six questions about God, Christ, Rama, Krishna, Brahma, Vishnu, Shiva and more. In October 1894, Rajchandra sent careful answers and books on Hinduism and recommended patience. 'Somewhat pacified', Gandhi remained a loyal Hindu who would however look at Hindu texts in the light of reason and morality.

The Gandhi who fought hard for Hindu temples to open their doors to long-excluded untouchables was not himself a temple-goer. Nor did he keep images of Hindu gods in his home or hut. Rama or Raam was his favourite name for God, but he was equally comfortable with Krishna, God, Khuda, Allah, or Yahweh, or any other name.

And although he often recalled a moral from the Ramayana, he did not see that text as history. 'The Rama whom I adore,' Gandhi explained, 'is God Himself,' different from any historical Rama. 'He always was, is now, and will be forever,' a God who was 'Unborn and Uncreated'.

This Eternal God of Gandhi did not have a special relationship with a geographical area. Gandhi's Hinduism was more moral than racial or national, and linked more to his soul than to the soil of India.

He approached this Eternal God through prayer both silent and voiced, and his multifaith prayers, joined by many, included short texts from different faiths as well as prayer songs from different traditions.

When William Stuart Nelson, Dean of Washington DC's Howard University, travelled to Noakhali in January 1947 to meet him, Gandhi the Hindu got Nelson to sing a Christian song, 'O God Our Help in Ages Past', to a largely Muslim audience in the village of Srirampur, which Gandhi translated. If we imagine that scene, we get an idea of Gandhi's God.

∎

In 1928 Gandhi offered this rhythmic declaration of his faith in God:

> In the midst of death, life persists; in the midst of untruth, truth persists; in the midst of darkness, light persists. Hence I gather that God is Life, Truth, Light. He is Love. He is the Supreme Good.

Among the many witnesses Gandhi invoked to prove God's love were India's poet-saints like Kabir, Nanak, Tulsidas, Chaitanya, Narsi Mehta, and Tukaram and Paul of Tarsus, whose First Letter to the Corinthians was among Gandhi's favourite texts.

And though he spoke of longings to attain perfection, Gandhi always identified himself with petitioners to the Almighty who saw themselves as poor sinners. At the peak of his huge Non-cooperation Movement of 1921, Gandhi called himself 'a weak, frail, miserable being'.

Often he spoke of a God who directly and personally aided human beings, as in Abbottabad, the Frontier Province, in July 1939:

The greatest of things in this world are accomplished not through unaided human effort.

Or, as he said in 1945:

[God is] proving for me His greatness and goodness every day… I can't even count the blessings; they are so many. For even the so-called sorrows and pains He sends descend like blessings.

Or as he put it in Noakhali on 10 Jan 1947, speaking to his grand-niece and helper, Manu:

Just observe how God sustains me. Though I sleep at 10 or 11 p.m., rise at 2 or 2.30 a.m., do my work at high pressure and get no rest at all, I carry on somehow. That itself is a wonder.

In the pre-dawn hours of 1 June 1947, having woken up earlier than usual, he mused on his isolation from men like Nehru and Patel, loyal colleagues for thirty years who had now opted for the partition he had deeply disliked. Manu recorded his words:

Today I find myself all alone… But somehow in spite of my being all alone, in my thoughts I am experiencing an ineffable inner joy and freshness of mind. I feel as if God himself was lighting my path before me. [Which is] why I am able to fight on single-handed.

On 18 January 1948, after ending his last fast, Gandhi explained why instead of 'God' he spoke at times of 'Truth':

I embarked on the fast in the name of Truth whose familiar name is God… In the name of God we have indulged in lies, massacres of people, without caring whether they were innocent or guilty, men or women, children or infants. We have indulged in abductions, forcible conversions and we have done all this shamelessly. I am not aware if anybody has done these things in the name of Truth. With that same name on my lips I have broken the fast.

About an earlier fast, in 1933, he said more than once that an inner voice he heard had urged him to undertake it. His close associate Vinoba Bhave probed him on this:

> You have said that Truth is God; but you have also said that during your fast, you heard the inner voice. Now what was that?
>
> He answered: 'Yes, there was something like that. It was not anything usual. I heard the voice clearly.' I asked: what should I do? The answer was, 'You should fast.' I asked, 'For how long?' The reply was, 'For 21 days.'
>
> He said, 'I felt God was talking to me.' I said, 'Does God have a form?' He replied, 'If a voice can be heard, perhaps the face too can be seen.' But he admitted he had not seen God.

•

The Cross was a magnet for Gandhi.

In October 1946, after violence had erupted in Noakhali and two of his Bengali associates, Satis Chandra Dasgupta, a scientist and inventor, and Satin Sen, expressed willingness to assist in Noakhali, Gandhi spoke to them of 'Jesus's example' of 'perfect sacrifice':

> A man who was completely innocent offered himself as a sacrifice for the good of others, including his enemies, and became the ransom of the world. It was a perfect act. 'It is finished' were the last words of Jesus, and we have the testimony of his four disciples as to its authenticity. But whether the Jesus tradition is historically true or not, I do not care.

A year later, on 26 October 1947, when Gandhi was striving to bring security to its Muslims, and some Hindu groups spoke freely of their dislike of Gandhi, he said the following to a group of Delhi's Muslim leaders who kept him posted day after day on their community's situation:

> Jesus Christ prayed to God from the Cross to forgive those

who had crucified him. It is my constant prayer to God that He may give me the strength to intercede even for my assassin. And it should be your prayer too that your faithful servant may be given that strength to forgive.

■

This champion of nonviolence, love and forgiveness was not however a pacifist. Not only did he take part, albeit with an ambulance corps, in the suppression of violence in Zululand, he raised an ambulance corps for World War I, and even tried to recruit Indian soldiers for that war. In 1942, when he mounted the Quit India campaign, that campaign promised that a free India would permit Allied troops to remain in India to prosecute the war.

True, he did on occasion say, in October 1939 for example, that 'it is better for India to discard violence altogether even for defending her borders'. However, shortly after independence, when Afridi tribesmen armed and equipped by the Pakistani army marched into Kashmir, and the Indian government sent troops to protect Kashmir, Gandhi, in his own words, gave 'tacit support' to the action.

Yet in July 1940 Gandhi had asked the British people to let Hitler 'take possession of their land and oppose the Nazis solely with nonviolent non-cooperation'. This was purely theoretical advice, rendered in the context of a dispute within the Indian National Congress on whether or not to accept a vague British offer of possible future independence provided the Congress enlisted in the War.

Convinced that Prime Minister Churchill had no intention to let go of India, Gandhi also argued that a deal with the Empire would militarize India. When pro-deal colleagues led by Rajagopalachari asked, 'Can Hitler be opposed without arms?' Saying 'Yes,' Gandhi went on to make that unrealistic suggestion to the British people.

This was the professor of nonviolence underlining its universal applicability in order to buttress his practical advice against accepting what he thought was an insincere offer from the Empire.

After the War ended and independence too had come, Gandhi publicly complimented Churchill for leading his country in World War II. This was seven years after he had given his theoretical advice to the British. There was 'no doubt', Gandhi said on 28 September 1947, that Churchill, who 'took the helm when Great Britain was in great danger', had 'saved the British Empire'. As Gandhi well knew, Churchill had done so with guns and bombs.

There were moments when the voice of ahimsa and the voice of the leader of India's independence movement did not coincide. The inconsistent Mahatma was also a very human, and very Indian, Mohandas Gandhi.

CHAPTER 4

HIS VEXED RELATIONSHIP WITH
CHURCHILL

India's confrontation with the British Empire is fascinatingly revealed in Gandhi's relationship with Winston Churchill, his opposite number in the Empire. This chapter examines that relationship as also Gandhi's strategies for the attainment of independence.

Churchill would have first heard of Gandhi in 1899-1900, when he was a war correspondent in South Africa. In a book he wrote thereafter, *My African Journey*, Churchill said that the interests of the Indians and the British in South Africa were 'irreconcilable'. Suggesting that 'Asiatics' might 'teach the African natives evil ways', Churchill added that the white man in South Africa believed 'he could strike down [the Indian immigrant] with his hands'.

That remark could well have been a description of an incident in Durban in 1897, two years before Churchill's arrival in South Africa, when a white mob very nearly lynched a twenty-seven-year-old Gandhi.

Nine years after that incident, Churchill, who was younger by five years, and Gandhi met for the first and last time in London. Churchill was colonial secretary and Gandhi had journeyed to England to seek imperial protection for South Africa's Indians.

This 1906 interview was cordial enough, but the torchbearers of Empire and Swaraj were fated to clash.

A quarter century later, in February 1931, when Lord Irwin, the viceroy, invited Gandhi to the Empire's grand new mansion in New Delhi to talk about possible dominion status for India, Churchill uttered his famous alarm that 'a seditious Middle Temple lawyer now posing as a fakir' was 'striding half-naked up the steps of the viceregal palace to parley on equal terms with the king-emperor'. Churchill had made a minor mistake: Gandhi's law studies in London took place at the Inner Temple, not the Middle Temple.

A month later, after Irwin accepted some of Gandhi's demands, and Gandhi agreed to attend a conference in London, Churchill protested in the House of Commons that Gandhi and the Indian National Congress had been 'raised to a towering pedestal', and appeasement offered to those inflicting 'such humiliation and defiance...as has not been known since the British first trod the soil of India'.

During that London conference of 1931, Gandhi talked with every major British leader and had tea with the King, but Churchill turned down Gandhi's requests to meet him.

In his utterances in England, Gandhi did not hide his goal:

The object of our nonviolent movement...is complete independence for India, not in any mystic sense but in the English sense of the term... I feel that every country is entitled to it without any question of its fitness or otherwise. As every country is fit to eat, to drink and to breathe, even so is every nation fit to manage its affairs, no matter how badly.

Ten years later, in August 1941, Churchill, now prime minister, referred to the Atlantic Charter for national independence and spoke of more than a dozen countries in Europe and Asia where independence was lost or threatened. But on India he remained silent. And in November of 1942, after Gandhi's Quit India call and arrest earlier that year, Churchill declared that he had 'not become the King's First Minister in order to preside over the liquidation of the British Empire'.

Churchill was not pleased when the viceroy, Lord Wavell, released Gandhi on health grounds in May 1944. Eight weeks later, according to Wavell's diary, the Prime Minister sent him 'a peevish telegram to ask why Gandhi hadn't died yet.'

In the summer of 1945, the British people voted out the victor of their war against Germany. Though no longer prime minister, Churchill exhorted Viceroy Wavell to 'keep a bit of India' even if independence was unavoidable; he also asked for India to be broken up into 'Pakistan, Hindustan and Princestan'.

After Independence and Partition, when carnage occurred in both halves of Punjab, Winston Churchill, now in the Opposition, underscored Gandhi's shame in a speech on 27 September 1947:

> The fearful massacres which are occurring in India are no surprise to me. We are, of course, only at the beginning of these horrors and butcheries, perpetrated upon one another, with the ferocity of cannibals, by the races gifted with capacities for the highest culture, and who had for generations dwelt, side by side, in general peace, under the broad, tolerant and impartial rule of the British Crown and Parliament. I cannot but doubt, that the future will witness a vast abridgment of the [subcontinent's] population.

To these formidable phrases from his old foe, Gandhi, who had arrived in Delhi from eastern India and hoped to go to Punjab, offered an immediate and pretty remarkable response.

Speaking to those present at his prayer meeting on 28 September, he first translated into Hindi Churchill's strong and hurtful sentences. Next he called the former premier 'a great man', adding, as we've seen, that there was 'no doubt' that Churchill, who 'took the helm when Great Britain was in great danger', had 'saved the British Empire' in World War II, and admitted that 'a few [hundred thousand persons] in India had taken to the path of barbarism'.

Then he took Churchill to task for describing the killings in India with, as Gandhi put it, 'such relish and gross exaggeration', and asked Churchill 'to take the trouble' of thinking about Britain's responsibility in the tragedy.

Though not referring to Churchill's personal wish for India's breakup, Gandhi added that by dividing India before quitting, Britain had 'unwittingly invited the two parts of the country to fight each other', a step 'the future may or may not justify'. He concluded by saying to his people:

> Many of you have given grounds to Mr. Churchill for making such remarks. You still have sufficient time to...prove Mr. Churchill's prediction wrong.

■

The weapon of satyagraha enabled the people of India to go beyond petitioning, which was humiliating and mostly fruitless, and bomb-throwing, which only provoked more repression. Satyagraha also baffled the Empire. Repressing nonviolent demonstrators invited outrage, but permitting them to defy the law eroded imperial prestige.

Between 1917 and 1942, Gandhi initiated numerous localized or nationwide satyagrahas:

- against oppression by European planters of indigo-growers in Bihar in 1917;
- against land tax in Gujarat's Kheda district in 1918;
- for higher wages for textile workers in Ahmedabad in 1918;
- across India in 1919 against curbs on free speech;
- in 1919-20 for action against the perpetrators of the Amritsar massacre;
- in 1920-22 for support to India's Muslims offended that Muslim holy places in the Middle East had passed from Turkish to European control;
- the nationwide defiance of the tax on salt in 1930;
- an all-India defiance in 1932-33 of restrictions on gatherings;
- individual disobedience across India of curbs on freedom of speech in 1940-41;
- and, finally, the nationwide Quit India stir of 1942.

Imperial will weakened from this succession of blows, and India gained independence. Other factors too were at work, including wars that consumed British resources and energies, as well as efforts of Indians willing to use violence. But the Empire's chief guardians conceded the major role played by satyagraha.

In achieving these results, Gandhi was aided by his flair, like that of a brilliant general, for knowing where to strike, when to strike, when to stop and regroup, and when to attack again.

■

Gandhi's incessant reminders to the people of India that their fight was against specific curbs, and against British rule, but *not* against the British people were often though not always heeded.

Rejecting the option of whipping up hatred against the British, Gandhi had written in 1925, 'I cannot love Muslims or Hindus and hate Englishmen,' and added, 'by a long course of prayerful discipline, I have ceased for over forty years to hate anybody'. A year later, he asked all Indians to reflect on the question:

> *15 July 1926:* We cannot love one another if we hate Englishmen. We cannot love the Japanese and hate Englishmen. We must either let the law of love rule us through and through or not at all. Love among ourselves based on hatred of others breaks down under the slightest pressure...

In 1931, when he spent a few months in England immediately after the triumphant disobedience over salt that so offended Churchill, the British people, including workers in Lancashire hurt by Indian boycotts, gave him a welcome that contrasted starkly with popular British reactions to the 1857 Revolt, which had seen gruesome violence, including by Indians.

At that time, reprisal, vengeance, and subduing the savage Oriental were popular cries in England. Making a private remark that would become unforgettable, Charles Dickens wrote in a letter on 4 October 1857:

I wish I were Commander-in-Chief in India... I should do
my utmost to exterminate the Race upon whom the stain of
the late cruelties rested.

If English reactions to Indian defiance had changed since then, a
major reason was the nonviolent nature of rebellions that Gandhi
had led. In 1931, many in Britain remembered his stoppage in 1922
of a great nationwide movement after angry Indians mercilessly
killed twenty-two of the Empire's Indian police in Chauri Chaura
in eastern United Provinces (as Uttar Pradesh was called until 1950),
a withdrawal resented at the time by many in the nonviolent army.

Then there was Gandhi's insistence that the British had to be
understood not as a single category but as a nation of different
individuals. This was a sharp departure, for in India's long history,
alien conquerors had again and again been dismissed as an uncivilized
homogeneous mass not deserving curiosity, study or differentiation.

Written at the end of the twelfth century, when Muhammad
Ghori attacked India, the Sanskrit poem *Prithvirajavijaya* described
in the following words a visit by Ghori's ambassador to the court
of the north Indian king, Prithviraj:

The colour of his beard, his eyebrows, his very lashes was
yellower than the grapes that grow in his native region...
Horrible was his speech, like the cry of wild birds; all his
phonemes were impure, impure as his complexion... He had
what looked like skin disease, so ghastly white he was...

Even if his phonemes were terrible, the ambassador had at least learnt
the Indian language used in Prithviraj's court. By contrast, Indians
were unwilling, not only in his time but for centuries thereafter, to
learn the supposedly barbaric language of an invader.

Our Gandhi, however, not only learnt the English language, as
did many of his compatriots, he also looked at the British people as
individuals. He separated a person from a demographic mass.

This was not necessarily the case with his colleagues. When

Gandhi and Vallabhbhai Patel were together in an imperial prison in 1932, Patel referred to British diehards and said of the British prime minister at the time, Ramsay McDonald, 'They are all birds of the same feather.' Gandhi disagreed, observing, 'Still I think [MacDonald] has his own convictions.'

After an English official, the commissioner of Poona, made a routine visit to the prisoners, Gandhi told Patel that the commissioner's casual remarks merited reflection, for they 'echo[ed] the table-talk of the ruling class'. To Gandhi, the British were a sum of individuals each of whom deserved careful attention, even if they frequently held similar views.

And more than attention. We have seen that Gandhi wanted the Indian people to fight but also love the British. As a result, India under Gandhi presented to the world a new if strange way of fighting.

Moreover, the free India of Gandhi's vision was ready, if there was equality and no subordination, to partner with England and the West for global purposes. Two months before his death, Gandhi imagined 'a new and robust India, not warlike...learning the best that the West has to give and becoming the hope not only of Asia and Africa, but of the whole of the aching world'.

■

Gandhi's chief challenge, in fact, was not the Empire's might but India's infighting. When in 1945 Churchill asked Wavell to split India into three or more parts, he was merely repeating a strategy that Rudyard Kipling, poet of the Empire, had spelt out more than thirty years earlier. In a 1911 history book aimed at British 'boys and girls interested in the story of Great Britain and her Empire' and co-authored by C. L. R. Fletcher, Kipling underlined the usefulness of India's divisions:

> The extension of our rule over the whole Indian peninsula was made possible, first by the exclusion of any other European power, and secondly by the fact that the weaker states and

princes continually called in our help against the stronger. From our three starting-points of Calcutta, Madras, and Bombay, we have gradually swallowed the whole country.

Asserting that Britain had suppressed the 1857 rebels with the help of Indian groups such as 'the gallant Sikhs and the Ghoorkas', Kipling added that three factors blocked Indian 'nationalism' in the post-1857 period: Muslim fear of Hindu rule; opposition by 'the native Princes'; and the 'complete indifference of the vast majority of the agricultural populations'.

He could have added a fourth obstacle: the 'untouchables' who saw no gain in high-caste Hindus replacing whites as India's ruling class.

Given these realities, as important as the weapon of satyagraha, and just as unexpected, was Gandhi's success in uniting bitterly divided Indians. Everyone knows that this success was incomplete: India *was* partitioned in 1947. Yet a historian may conclude that but for Gandhi's counter strategies, the Empire would have succeeded in using India's diversity to prevent Indian independence or greatly delay it.

Gandhi answered Kipling by bidding to make all in India Indians, and by affiliating himself to Indians in their entirety rather than to *his* Indian section or sections: Gujaratis, Banias and Hindus. If he *had* to focus on *portions* of the population, Gandhi would select the peasants and the poor, who were the great majority and who crossed borders of caste, language and religion.

India had seen impressive political leaders before Gandhi. Some worked as hard as him and gave more rousing speeches. But their focus usually was either on an unpopular British officer in their area, or on *their* caste or community in *their* region, for whose political leadership they strove.

From the day of his return to India in January 1915, Gandhi focused not on the 'enemy' (the British) nor on 'natural allies' (Gujaratis of his caste), but on the common people of all of India, and sought to tap their power.

Unlike other politicians, Gandhi had seen (from the start of his South African days) the interconnectedness, practical and moral, of three issues: independence, Hindu-Muslim understanding, and untouchability. Hindus would not *deserve* freedom from alien rule if they continued to treat a portion among them as untouchables; and caste Hindus were unlikely to *obtain* Swaraj if 'untouchables' opposed it. Similarly, if they fought each other, Hindus and Muslims would neither *merit* nor *attain* independence.

Gandhi understood, too, the necessity of finding the right pace on the three battlefronts. Patient work would be needed to attract Muslims and the untouchables onto the road to Swaraj. Yet he could not afford to be outflanked by Hindu militants tempting the influential Hindu high castes with an early Swaraj won via the bomb, a Swaraj, moreover, that the high castes would dominate; or, on the other wing, by Muslim extremists offering a revival of Muslim supremacy; or by radical foes of caste presenting dreams of instant equality among Indians, if necessary, under British auspices. His thrusts should not be premature, nor his caution excessive.

Moreover, luck favoured Gandhi. In South Africa, he found Indians of all kinds and backgrounds with whom he could work. Encountering there an India in miniature, he built links with caste Hindus, untouchables, Muslims from different sects, Sikhs, Parsis, Christians, Hindi-speakers from UP and Bihar, Tamils, Telugus, and others. He found openings not available to leaders confined, say, to Bengal, Maharashtra, UP or South India.

Applying some of these lessons soon after arriving in India, Gandhi initiated his first satyagraha not in his native Gujarat but in in far-off Bihar, on behalf of humble peasants growing indigo for European planters in Champaran. That Champaran exercise won major relief for the peasants. Moreover, news of its success brought Bihar closer to all parts of India and enhanced Indian-ness. Similar things happened after other battles in which Gandhi became involved.

In another major accomplishment, Gandhi not only transformed the Indian National Congress organizationally, a fact previously noted; he also widened its goals. From 1920, when Gandhi and the Congress became synonymous, Hindu-Muslim unity and the removal of untouchability became part of the political agenda of the Congress, along with independence.

∎

Also valuable for the national movement was Gandhi's ability to seize the moral high ground. When, in December 1919, four years after Gandhi's return to India, the Indian National Congress met for a plenary in Amritsar, the city which eight months earlier had witnessed the historic massacre ordered by Brigadier General Reginald Dyer, Gandhi drafted a resolution condemning the massacre but criticizing also the preceding violence in which five young Englishmen were killed and an Englishwoman assaulted.

A thirty-two-year-old Bombay lawyer and writer who was a delegate in Amritsar, K. M. Munshi, who later held senior positions in independent India, recorded the heated discussion on this resolution. The persons mentioned in Munshi's account are well known in Indian political history; the Mrs Besant he speaks of was the famous Annie Besant, the Irishwoman who had made India her home, and Indian home rule her mission.

> The hearts of most of us [Munshi would report] revolted at the latter part of the resolution... This must have been Mrs. Besant's work, many thought; she was after all British. One Punjab leader gave expression to the feeling rather crudely: no one born of an Indian mother, said he, could have drafted this resolution. Lokamanya [Tilak] too was indignant and so were [Bipin Chandra] Pal and C. R. Das; and the latter part of the resolution was lost by an overwhelming majority.
>
> The next day the President wanted the committee to reconsider the resolution as Gandhiji, he said, was very keen on it. There were vehement protests. Ultimately Gandhiji [who was unwell] was helped to the table to move that the resolution

be reconsidered. He spoke sitting. Out of respect the house sat quiet but with ill-concealed impatience.

Referring to the remark that no son born of an Indian mother could have drafted the resolution, Gandhiji stated that he had considered deeply and for long whether as an Indian he could have drafted the resolution, for indeed he had drafted it. But after long searching of the heart, he had come to the conclusion that only a person born of an Indian mother could have drafted it.

And then he spoke as if his whole life depended upon the question... When he stopped, we were at his feet... The resolution was reconsidered and accepted in its original form.

According to Munshi, 'the old guard were routed' at Amritsar and 'Gandhiji was left in possession of the field'. More importantly, Gandhi had given a new meaning to Indian honour, enabled the Congress to capture the moral heights, and put the Empire on the defensive.

■

Of the ten satyagrahas earlier listed, only one carried a religious tinge: the demand after the end of World War I that the Empire allay the resentment of India's Muslims at European control over Islam's holy places in the Middle East. The other nine satyagrahas were all totally secular, and the one of which the world took the greatest notice was the Salt March of 1930.

Let us look at the Salt March. At the end of December 1929, the Congress, meeting in Lahore (which would become part of Pakistan in 1947) resolved on a fresh round of civil disobedience but was unable to select the ground on which to offer battle.

Some wanted the land tax lowered. Others proposed marches on imperial buildings. Picketing of liquor shops was suggested. Subhas Bose asked for the creation of a parallel government.

As the founder of satyagraha, Gandhi was asked to pick the issue. After about five weeks, he came up with salt, or rather the tax on it.

The Empire's officers were not the only ones to chuckle over salt. Jawaharlal Nehru, his father Motilal, Vallabhbhai Patel, and other prominent leaders in Congress were shocked. One Congress leader asked if the fly of the Salt Act deserved the hammer of satyagraha. India's leading British-owned journal, *The Statesman* of Calcutta, wrote:

> There is something almost childishly theatrical in challenging in this way the salt monopoly of the Government.

The world knows that the last laugh belonged to Gandhi. He had chosen salt because it was basic to life, because the tax on it affected every Indian—Hindu, Muslim, female, male, untouchable, high caste, whatever—and especially the poor, and in every part of India. And because defying the law was simple: all you had to do was to pick up salt from anywhere on India's long seashore or buy or sell illegally collected salt anywhere in the land.

The evening before his march was to begin from his Ahmedabad ashram, Gandhi spelt out the magic of nonviolent defiance:

> Supposing I had announced I was going to launch a violent campaign...do you think the Government would have left me free until now? Can you show me an example in history, be it England, America or Russia, where the State has tolerated violent defiance of authority for a single day? But here you know that the Government is puzzled and perplexed.
>
> Supposing ten men in each of the 700,000 villages in India come forward to manufacture salt and to disobey the Salt Act, what...can this Government do? Even the worst autocrat you can imagine would not dare to blow regiments of peaceful resisters out of a cannon's mouth.

On 12 March 1930, Gandhi and seventy-eight carefully chosen colleagues began their 220-mile walk from Ahmedabad to Dandi, through several villages and towns, which too were carefully chosen. Many Indians employed by the government in villages along the route resigned their jobs, and hundreds followed the marchers from their village to the next.

For days the Empire hesitated to arrest Gandhi: it was afraid of unmanageable unrest. Moreover, Gandhi had not yet violated any law.

Reaching Dandi on 5 April, he scooped up a fistful of salt from the sand, thereby breaking the law and releasing a spring.

Thousands followed him, picking up salt on the west coast, on the east coast, in Bengal, in the Tamil country, and elsewhere. The ranks of peaceful satyagrahis swelled. In the hinterland, thousands bought or sold contraband salt.

Far to the north of Ahmedabad, Pashtuns of the Northwestern Province, led by the remarkable Abdul Ghaffar Khan, the imposing founder of the nonviolent army of Khudai Khidmatgars, violated a law banning assembly and stood up before the government's horses, sticks, and machine guns. Ordered to open fire at unarmed Pashtuns, the Empire's Garhwal Rifles disobeyed the order, thereby staging *their* revolt.

As Churchill would soon lament, the authority of the Empire had taken a nosedive. It had plunged in front of an intrigued world kept informed by reporters flocking to India. Gandhi and close to a hundred thousand Indians were placed behind bars for six months or longer, but the India-Empire equation had changed forever.

The Canadian scholar George Woodcock has said:

In his superb sense of timing, in his quick intuitive grasp of the balance of forces, in his instinct for effective symbolic action, and in his grasp of the strategy of struggle, Gandhi was one of the most able politicians of his time.

This excellent summation leaves out a major accomplishment of the Salt satyagraha: through it, hundreds of thousands of Indians, men, women and the young, conquered the fear of being beaten or imprisoned.

Two other aspects of the Salt March should be noted. In villages on his route, Gandhi fraternized with the untouchables, bathed in water from 'impure' untouchable wells, embarrassing and offending high-caste reception committees.

Secondly, women joined the struggle in growing numbers. Frederick Sykes, the Bombay governor facing the brunt of Gandhi's march, said in a letter to Viceroy Irwin:

> There is no doubt that Gandhi has a great emotional hold...
> The popular enthusiasm, largely among the younger generation
> and increasingly amongst women and girls...has been more
> than was expected.

Before reaching Dandi, Gandhi wrote these lines, now well known, about women:

> To call woman the weaker sex is a libel; it is man's injustice to
> woman... If by strength is meant moral power, then woman
> is immeasurably man's superior. Has she not greater intuition,
> is she not more self-sacrificing, has she not greater powers of
> endurance, has she not greater courage?... If nonviolence is the
> law of our being, the future is with woman.

■

Among the numerous leaders of national movements for independence in Asia and Africa after World War II ended, Gandhi was the *only one* not to assume office when freedom was won. He had opted for this abstinence years earlier. On 6 March 1931, just after the famous Gandhi-Irwin Pact was signed, the following exchange took place in New Delhi:

> *Journalist:* Do you expect Purna Swaraj (Complete Independence)
> in your lifetime?
> *Gandhi:* I do look for it most decidedly. I still consider myself
> a young man of sixty-two.
>
> *Journalist:* Would you agree to become the Prime Minister of
> the future government?

Gandhi: No. It will be reserved for younger minds and stouter hearts.

For some time he had been thinking of the future, which was one reason why in 1929 he declined the presidency of the Congress to which he was voted, and instead proposed the name of forty-year-old Jawaharlal Nehru, who did become president.

At the end of 1930, when a new president was needed, and Vithalbhai Patel, who chaired the Central Assembly in Delhi but had lately joined the ranks of the satyagrahis, pressed his claim, Gandhi threw his weight behind Patel's younger brother Vallabhbhai, who became the new president, with Jawaharlal as the general secretary.

Much later, in November 1947, after India had become independent, and again thinking for the future, Gandhi proposed young Jayaprakash Narayan for Congress president. Prime Minister Nehru and Deputy Prime Minister Patel jointly and successfully opposed the idea, yet what this episode recalls is old Gandhi's interest in the future of the Congress and therefore in younger leaders.

We looked earlier at Gandhi's role, begun in 1919, in creating a nationwide and multi-level structure for the Congress. It seems legitimate to see his lifelong interest in the health of the Congress as part of his concern for the future of independent India's democracy.

When in 1915 he first involved himself with the Congress, that body was divided between moderates and extremists. Next, in the 1920s and 1930s, came a division between the Congress's anti-Empire hardliners and those seeing benefits in negotiating with it. From the early 1930s, the Congress also contained an active Socialist group which clashed with those who recognized the reality and value of the better-off, as also of the market.

From the 1920s, there was a running conflict inside the Congress between those wanting to take struggle and satyagraha to the princely states that formed a large portion of India's land where, secure under the imperial umbrella, rajas and nawabs ruled, often in autocratic fashion, and others cautious about pushing these influential princes even more deeply into British hands.

In the late 1930s, when for two years elected Congress ministers enjoyed a share of real power in most of India's provinces, even as the centre remained in British hands, there were sharp disputes between those believing that power would aid the cause of freedom, and others worried that office would soften freedom fighters and turn them into defenders of Empire.

And the last year of Gandhi's life saw a divide between those committed to an India that provided equal rights to all, and others who felt that in an India shorn of its Muslim-majority parts, Hindus ought to enjoy the privileged position that was being sought for Muslims in Pakistan.

Each of these divides was real and sharp and capable of splitting the Congress. In a remarkable and usually overlooked feat, Gandhi managed to bridge or manage every one of these perilous divides.

Sometimes he used shock treatment, as in 1934, when he decided to retire from the Congress. The years from 1932 to 1934 had seen great repression from the government. Most including Gandhi had been in and out of prison. There were sharp differences within the Congress on how to respond to the repression.

In a letter (5 September 1934) addressed to Patel—the last elected president of the Congress—Gandhi explained that many who differed from him suppressed their views. Seeing himself as a 'stifling' force 'arresting [the] full play of reason', he would resign to promote free discussion.

At this point of time, prominent Congress figures Patel, Rajagopalachari and Prasad, all three holding conservative economic views, nursed sharp misgivings about the socialists. Nehru sympathized with the latter but was in prison.

Feeling a bond with all these colleagues, Gandhi concluded that the best way of not lending his weight to any one side was for him to leave the Congress. The two groups should fend for themselves, if necessary have it out with one another, and find their levels. If need arose, he would work from outside to unite the groups.

There was also his advancing age, plus physical attacks on his person from orthodox elements infuriated by Gandhi's campaigns against untouchability and for Hindu-Muslim understanding. The Congress should learn to think of a future without him.

Finally, Gandhi sensed that his retirement might facilitate a settlement between the Congress and the Empire. If this did not come about, and another clash proved necessary, the Congress could always summon him to lead it.

Maulana Azad, a prominent figure who had presided over the Congress in 1923 and would do so again from 1940 to 1946, protested against Gandhi's step, and a disconcerted Rajagopalachari argued that Gandhi would 'surely be disappointed' if he thought that he could retire and still keep the Congress or himself 'politically important'.

In fact Gandhi was being astute. His retirement would enable the Congress to present a cooperating face to the Empire while the chief rebel remained in the wings, available, when the time came, to resume fighting.

Gandhi was not breaking with the Congress, only redefining his relationship with it, yet sending the resignation letter gave him a pang. 'It is not with a light heart,' he wrote, 'that I leave this great organization'. To the October 1934 session in Bombay, chaired by Rajendra Prasad, Gandhi said:

> I am not going out as a protest against anything inside the Congress. I am going out so that Congressmen may think and act for themselves. My retirement does not in any way mean that I am not ready to come back whenever my help is needed.
>
> I am leaving the Congress to lift the weight which has been suppressing it, in order that it may grow, and I may grow myself... I am leaving in order to develop the power that non-violence has...
>
> If you have given me the position of a general commanding an army, you must allow that general to judge whether he serves the army by being at its head or whether he serves the army by

retiring and giving place to lieutenants who have served well.
If you believe that I have been a fairly wise general, you
must believe in my judgement even now...

■

Recreating and streamlining the Congress, fusing it with India's
peasants and workers, turning it into a fighting machine, and keeping
it united, Gandhi had become one with the Congress. Later we will
see that near the end of his life Gandhi felt disappointed with it
and proposed a radical next step. Here we must pause to recognize
that even on its finest day the Congress could not possibly represent
all of the Indian people.

India was simply too large, too populous, too varied, and too
divided to be fully represented by one organization, no matter how
remarkable or wisely guided. To put it differently, not everyone in
India felt that 'complete independence for India in the English sense
of the term' or 'getting out of alien control'—to recall two of
Gandhi's phrases from 1931—was their chief or sole goal.

There were many groups in India who resented other Indian
groups more than alien rule; and if Gandhi felt called to liberate
India from the Empire, others felt a calling to liberate or protect
their group from a larger and more powerful Indian group.

And if Churchill was Gandhi's opposite number in the Empire,
a man like Muhammad Ali Jinnah, seven years younger than Gandhi,
saw the latter, during phases in his life, as an opposite number from
whom his people, as he saw them, the Muslims of India, had to
be saved.

Likewise, a man like Bhimrao Ramji Ambedkar, twenty-two years
younger than Gandhi, also saw the latter, during phases in his life, as
someone from whom his people, as he saw them, the untouchables
or Dalits of India, had to be saved.

Just as Gandhi was an admirer of Empire until he became its
unrelenting foe, both Jinnah and Ambedkar were Gandhi's admirers

until they became his unrelenting foes.

The stories of their relationship with Gandhi, and of the relationship of the Muslims of India with the rest of India, and of Dalits with caste Hindus, and of how Gandhi addressed those questions, will be told in the next two chapters.

CHAPTER 5

THE LESSONS OF PARTITION

In this chapter we will look at Gandhi's unsuccessful attempt to preserve a united India, as also the goals and strategies of Muhammad Ali Jinnah, the fellow-Gujarati who, like Gandhi, studied law in London, and the role of other forces in the partition outcome.

India's Hindu-Muslim question began with Islam's arrival centuries ago.

From the twelfth century to the nineteenth, Muslim monarchs sat on Delhi's throne and from there ruled much or most of India. By about the fifteenth century, Muslims appeared to constitute a majority in the northwest and the east of the subcontinent—in Punjab, Sindh, Balochistan, Kashmir and the Northwest Frontier, and in Bengal.

However, Hindus remained a majority in the core area of India's Muslim kingdoms—the large region all around Delhi—as also in India as a whole. When the British left in 1947, Muslims constituted around 25 per cent of the subcontinent's population.

Over time, coexistence and interdependence became the norm, especially among the lower classes, who formed the majority. Coexistence and frequent participation in each other's festivals did not, however, lead to the creation of a single community.

■

The 1857 Revolt against British rule was fully crushed by 1859. While the Empire absorbed its lessons, Indians generally did not.

One major lesson was that Muslim-Hindu partnership had supplied energy to the Revolt.

From the late 1850s, an astute Empire carried forward its strategy of keeping Muslims, Hindus and Sikhs focused on their religious identity and divided from one another. This strategy was carefully implemented in the Empire's post-Revolt Indian armies. Charles Wood, secretary of state in London, wrote to Viceroy Canning in 1861: 'If one regiment mutinies, the next regiment [should be] so alien that it would be ready to fire into it.'

The strategy was also implemented politically. A solidly Muslim eastern Bengal province, created in 1905 by partitioning the Bengal presidency, disappeared in 1911 when, following large-scale agitation, the presidency was reunited, pleasing many Bengali Hindus as also the Indian National Congress, which had been formed in 1885.

In the meantime, in 1909, the Empire statutorily conceded a demand, first voiced in 1906 by a delegation of prominent Muslims, for a quota of Muslims seats in any councils, and an exclusive Muslim electorate for these seats.

In 1906, when Viceroy Minto assured the delegation that its demand for a separate electorate would have the Empire's support, an unnamed British official congratulated him right away:

> I must send Your Excellency a line to say that a very, very big thing has happened today. A work of statesmanship that will affect India and Indian history for many a long year. It is nothing less than the pulling back of 62 millions of people [India's Muslim population at the time] from joining the ranks of the seditious opposition [the Congress].

The year 1909 also saw the formation, in Dhaka, now the Bangladesh capital, of the All-India Muslim League.

One brilliant Muslim did *not* support a separate Muslim electorate at this point and did *not* join the Muslim League: Muhammad Ali Jinnah. His parents, like Gandhi's, belonged to Gujarat's Kathiawar region. Converted to Islam only a generation or two before he was born, Jinnah's family had joined Shia Islam's Ismaili or Khoja sect, led by the Aga Khan.

Like Gandhi, young Jinnah studied law in London. Like Gandhi, he seemed keen on Muslim-Hindu understanding. In 1913, after wars in the Balkans threatened Turkey, seen then as the world's principal Muslim power, Jinnah, already in the Congress and aspiring to be a bridge, joined the Muslim League as well.

The year 1909, when the Muslim League was founded and a separate Muslim electorate created, was also when Gandhi wrote his text *Hind Swaraj* on a ship from England back to South Africa. Although Gandhi would not return to India until 1915, this significant text was about India, not about Indians in South Africa.

Here is what Gandhi wrote about the Hindu-Muslim question in *Hind Swaraj* in 1909:

> If the Hindus believe that India should be peopled only by Hindus, they are living in dreamland. The Hindus, the Muslims, the Parsis and the Christians who have made India their country are fellow-countrymen, and they will have to live in unity, if only for their own interest.
>
> In no part of the world are one nationality and one religion synonymous terms; nor has it ever been so in India...
>
> Is the God of the Muslim different from the God of the Hindu?... There are deadly proverbs as between the followers of Siva and those of Vishnu, yet nobody suggests that these two do not belong to the same nation...
>
> Those who do not wish to misunderstand things may read up the Qur'an, and they will find therein hundreds of passages acceptable to the Hindus, and the Bhagavad Gita contains passages to which not a Muslim can take exception. Am I to dislike a Muslim because there are passages in the Qur'an I do not understand or like?

Until his death four decades later, these would remain Gandhi's steadfast views. Articulated one hundred and seven years ago, these thoughts seem directly relevant to our world today.

•

In 1915 Gandhi returned to India. At the end of 1916, he supported the historic Lucknow Pact between the Congress and the Muslim League under which the two bodies agreed to work jointly for Indian self-government, with the Congress giving up its opposition to a separate Muslim electorate.

Both parties also agreed to *weightage* for minorities, a policy for giving Hindus in Muslim-majority provinces and Muslims in Hindu-majority provinces a higher-than-proportional share in any councils.

This pact had three principal architects: Poona's Bal Gangadhar Tilak, who was staunch for the Hindu interest; Annie Besant, who would preside over the Congress in 1917; and Jinnah, a rising star in both the Congress and the League.

This Lucknow Pact found the two communities asking the Empire for the same thing. However, Muslims in undivided Punjab and reunited Bengal felt cheated by the pact, for in these two large Muslim-majority provinces weightage was likely to give non-Muslims a majority in the council.

Unlike the big Bombay and Madras presidencies, or the populous province of UP, where Muslims made up a small minority, or the Northwest Frontier, where non-Muslims comprised a tiny minority, Hindus and Sikhs in Punjab, and Hindus in Bengal, were *large* minorities, around 40 per cent of the population. Electoral weightage for them could deny Punjab and Bengal a Muslim chief.

This difficulty was overlooked during the years between 1919 and 1922, when the Gandhi-led Non-cooperation Movement brought together Hindus and Muslims, as also the Congress and the League. Jinnah was pushed offstage while the Ali Brothers, Shaukat and Muhammad, and Maulana Abul Kalam Azad became India's most prominent Muslim figures, standing alongside Gandhi.

When the Non-cooperation Movement seemed to peter out in the mid-1920s, Jinnah returned to centre stage and came up with another proposal for a Congress–League pact: Let the League accept joint electorates, and let the Congress agree to the removal of weightage in Punjab and Bengal.

Jinnah also asked that, for enhancing their sense of security, Muslims should receive a one-third share in any future Central Assembly, higher than their one-fourth ratio in the population.

From an all-India perspective, Jinnah's bold package was reasonable, even attractive. But Punjab's Hindus and Sikhs and Bengal's Hindus, better off than Muslims of their provinces in the economy and the professions, refused to touch it. They thought it was their toil, not anyone's favours, that had earned them their superior economic and social situation. As for political weightage, it was part of a contract.

Meeting in Calcutta at the end of 1928, the Congress and other groups yielded to these views and rejected Jinnah's proposal, while agreeing to a 27 per cent share for Muslims in a central legislature.

Gandhi was willing personally to accept Jinnah's terms but unable to bring around the Congress leaders of Bengal and Punjab. Although called a miracle worker between 1919 and 1922, he could not change ground realities in 1928.

The Calcutta outcome was shattering for Jinnah and for others hoping for a political settlement of the Hindu–Muslim question. Soon thereafter, Jinnah removed himself to London, to practice law there.

■

From London, Jinnah watched the Salt March and connected campaigns that shook India from 1930 to 1933, the Empire's tough reaction thereafter, and the Congress's response. In 1934, he returned to an India about to try out provincial autonomy, with the Empire hoping that office in provincial governments would soften Indian politicians, and the Congress hoping that provincial responsibility would lead one day to national power.

After provincial elections held in February 1937, the Congress formed ministries in eight provinces and with allies in Bombay, Assam, and the Muslim-majority province of the NWFP, where

Dr Khan Sahib headed the Congress-led alliance.

Except in the Frontier Province, however, the Congress received only a small share of the Muslim vote. Led by Jinnah, who was elected as 'permanent' president in 1934, the Muslim League, contesting for Muslim seats under the separate electorate performed well in Hindu-majority provinces, where it vowed to protect threatened Muslim interests, but not so well in Muslim-majority Punjab, Bengal, Sindh, and the NWFP, where Muslims did not view Hindus as a danger.

In mostly agricultural Punjab, where both the Congress and the Muslim League had remained essentially urban parties, the government—elected under a restricted franchise—was formed by the pro-Empire and pro-feudal Unionist Party, made up of Muslim, Sikh and Hindu landlords but also supported by many farmers. In Bengal, the League became part of a coalition ministry headed by the Peasants Party's Fazlul Huq.

Leading the Congress campaign early in 1937, Jawaharlal Nehru asked Indians to choose 'between the Congress and the British'. Jinnah replied: 'I refuse to line up. There is a third party—the Muslims. We are not going to be dictated to by anybody.'

The Empire/colony confrontation thus morphed from 1937 into a trickier, three-sided clash, involving the Empire, the Congress and the League, although there were other forces too, like the Unionist Party in Punjab.

Whereas the ideologically-driven Jawaharlal Nehru would not touch the feudal Unionists, Gandhi was willing to explore common ground with this regional party which espoused a Muslim-Sikh-Hindu partnership, as was the Congress leader in the south, the Madras Premier, Rajagopalachari. However, in 1941, a vigilant viceroy and his officers in Lahore prevented Rajagopalachari's overtures from reaching the Unionist Premier of Punjab, Sikander Hayat Khan.

From 1937 to 1939, the Congress, guided by Gandhi, played its cards skilfully, its ministries pleasing the public with popular measures and impressing the Empire with its discipline. What suddenly strengthened Jinnah's hand was Hitler's attack on Poland in September

1939, which started World War II.

Fought by the Allies in democracy's name, the War made the Indian people keener than ever for freedom, while making the Empire keener than before to delay it. As soon as War was declared, the British Parliament empowered the Viceroy in India, Lord Linlithgow, to override or take over India's provincial governments.

Gandhi's instincts told him that the Congress should show sympathy for Britain and the Allies, but the national mood was against any expression of support without a clear assurance of freedom after the War, which the Empire refused to give.

For formulating a united Indian response to the War, Gandhi invited Jinnah to join a discussion along with Congress leaders. On 9 September, he wrote in his journal *Harijan*:

> [I]n the midst of this catastrophe without parallel...Congressmen
> and all other responsible Indians individually and collectively
> have to decide what part India is to play in this terrible drama.

Declining Gandhi's invitation, Jinnah accepted the Viceroy's, for Linlithgow too was wooing him. Two years earlier, in 1937, Churchill had asked Linlithgow to build India's Muslims as 'a counter-check on Congress'. In October 1939, the Viceroy wrote to King George VI in England that he was working on Jinnah, on India's rajas and other opponents of the Congress. It was, said the Viceroy, 'a heavy and trying task, but well worth the trouble'.

'It has been decided,' the Viceroy added, that the Congress would not be given 'what they are asking for', namely 'an understanding... that India will [receive] political independence at the [end] of the war'.

Unwilling to serve as docile agents of a hardening Empire, all Congress ministries resigned in December 1939. Jinnah called the resignation 'deliverance' for Muslims.

In March 1940, Jinnah would say, 'Up to the time of the declaration of war, the Viceroy never thought of an important party... The Viceroy never thought of me.'

Whether he knew it or not, Hitler had stopped India's march to independence and produced an understanding between the Empire and the Muslim League.

．

This understanding quickly produced a far-reaching outcome. At the end of 1939, Viceroy Linlithgow suggested to Jinnah that the logical implication of his stand was a separate Muslim state, at which, as the Viceroy noted, Jinnah 'blushed'. The Viceroy also asked Zafrulla Khan, a member of his executive council, to draft a note advising the Muslim League to demand a separate nation.

The idea was not entirely novel. In 1930, the poet Iqbal had spoken of an autonomous Muslim entity in northwestern India, and in 1933 a Punjabi student at Cambridge University, Choudhry Rahmat Ali, had envisioned a future state he called 'Pakistan', to comprise Punjab, Sindh, Kashmir, Balochistan and the NWFP.

By January 1940 Jinnah was saying publicly that Hindus and Muslims were two different nations, and on 23 March separation was formally called for at a Muslim League session in Lahore.

From Punjab's soil, the Muslim League demanded 'separate and sovereign Muslim states, comprising geographically contiguous units...in which the Muslims are numerically in a majority, as in the north-western and eastern zones of India'.

The Bengal premier, Fazlul Huq of the peasant-championing Krishak Praja Party, heading a coalition ministry that included the Muslim League, moved the historic resolution, yet it was the Karachi-born Gujarati, Jinnah, who was Lahore's central figure. He was also a changed man, arousing passion, unlike the reasoning Jinnah of the 1920s. *The Times* of London reported that prolonged cheering almost drowned Jinnah's remark that he would 'give his life to achieve' a Muslim state.

Several equations too had suddenly changed, in Jinnah's favour: the League's equation with the Empire and the Congress; the League's equation with other bodies interested in Muslim support, including Punjab's Unionist Party and Bengal's peasants party; and Jinnah's equation with other Muslim leaders in India. Now the League leader could hope to avenge snubs he had received in 1937 from the Unionists in Punjab, the Krishak Praja Party in Bengal, and the Khudai Khidmatgars of the NWFP.

And avenge also an earlier upstaging, in 1920-22, by the Ali Brothers and Azad, and, most pleasing of all perhaps, avenge the sidelining in 1919-20 caused by Gandhi's emergence on the national stage.

■

The Lahore Resolution of 1940 did not ask for a homeland for India's Muslims, nor for removing all of the subcontinent's Muslims to one or two regions. It sought the separation from India of Muslim-majority areas. The boundaries of this Muslim-majority state were not specified in the Lahore Resolution, and there was also a clear suggestion (later dismissed as a typing error) that more than one Muslim state was being demanded.

Pointing out that the resolution, which was passed to sustained applause, did not describe the boundaries of the proposed new state, a delegate at Lahore said that its imprecise wording would encourage the partitioning of Punjab and Bengal, both of which contained large areas where non-Muslims comprised a majority. Liaquat Ali Khan, the League's general secretary, who belonged to Karnal in eastern Punjab, defended vagueness, saying:

> If we say 'Punjab,' that would mean that the boundary of our state would be Gurgaon, whereas we want to include in our proposed dominion Delhi and Aligarh, which are centres of our culture... Rest assured that we will [not] give away any part of the Punjab.

Ten days earlier, at Ramgarh in Bihar, where the Congress was meeting under Abul Kalam Azad's presidency, the Maulana drew a wholly different picture of the Hindu-Muslim relationship:

It was India's historic destiny that many human races and cultures and religions should flow to her, and that many a caravan should find rest here... One of the last of these caravans was that of the followers of Islam. This came here and settled here for good...

Everything bears the stamp of our joint endeavour. Our languages were different, but we grew to use a common language. Our manners and customs were different, but they produced a new synthesis... No fantasy or artificial scheming to separate and divide can break this unity.

To this Jinnah's response, given in Lahore, was that Hindus and Muslims could 'never evolve a common nationality' and that 'to yoke together two such nations under a single state' would destroy any fabric of government.

■

The Pakistan call was a frontal attack on Gandhi's vision. In written comments, Gandhi contested the doctrine behind it:

The 'Two Nations' theory is an untruth... Why is India not one nation? Was it not one during, say, the Moghul period? Is India composed of two nations? If it is, why only two? Are not Christians a third, Parsis a fourth, and so on? Are the Muslims of China a nation separate from the other Chinese? Are the Muslims of England a different nation from the other English?

How are the Muslims of the Punjab different from the Hindus and the Sikhs? Are they not all Punjabis, drinking the same water, breathing the same air and deriving sustenance from the same soil?

In practical terms, said Gandhi, it was 'worse than anarchy to partition a poor country like India whose every corner is populated by Hindus and Muslims living side by side'.

Yet Gandhi conceded that separation was possible:

If the vast majority of Indian Muslims feel that they are not
one nation with their Hindu and other brethren, who will be
able to resist them?

Pakistan cannot be worse than foreign domination. I have
lived under the latter though not willingly. If God so desires
it, I may have to become a helpless witness to the undoing
of my dream.

Gandhi also seemed to concede the principle of self-determination,
saying:

The Muslims must have the same right of self-determination
that the rest of India has. We are at present a joint family. Any
member may claim a division.

Five months later, however, in Bombay, Gandhi made emotional
remarks which appeared to contradict what he had said in April
and May:

I do not say this as a Hindu. I say this as a representative of
Hindus, Muslims, Parsis and all. I would say to Muslim brethren,
'Cut me to pieces first and then divide India. You are trying
to do something which was not attempted even during the
[Mughal] rule of 200 years. We shall not allow you to do it.'

■

In August 1940, with Churchill installed as prime minister, the Empire
declared from London that it could not assure Indian independence
after the war. It also promised never to allow India's minorities
to be 'coerced into submission' to a majority government. With
these announcements, the Muslim League, India's princes, and other
minority groups were given a veto over India's political future.

Four years later, in the summer of 1944, Gandhi, released after
twenty-one months in detention, explored a settlement with Jinnah
when several Congress leaders including the president, Azad, Nehru

and Patel were still in prison. After an exchange of letters, the two Gujaratis talked fourteen times in Bombay, between 9 and 27 September 1944.

For each meeting, Gandhi walked to Jinnah's house on Mount Pleasant Road in Malabar Hill. It was a short walk, for Gandhi too was staying on Mount Pleasant Road, in the house of his friends, the Birlas.

Both were unwell, with amoebae bothering Gandhi, who was close to his seventy-fifth birthday, and a sixty-seven-year-old Jinnah privately diagnosed with a more serious illness, 'unresolved pneumonia in the base of his lungs'.

Politically Jinnah was stronger than he had ever been. In 1944 the League claimed two million members; seventeen years earlier its membership had been less than 1,400.

Journalists crowded Jinnah's lawns and those of Birla House. Indians saw pictures of the two leaders smiling and meeting repeatedly. Gandhi sent to Jinnah his nature cure doctor and, on Eid day, which fell during the talks, a supply of wheat crackers.

Gandhi also made a concrete offer: if the Muslim League joined the Congress in asking for a national government, he would get the Congress to accept post-independence plebiscites for separation in the subcontinent's Muslim-majority areas. If the votes favoured separation, India and Pakistan should create bonds of alliance, Gandhi added.

But the talks failed. Objecting that Gandhi's Pakistan was not large enough, for it excluded the Muslim-minority areas of Punjab and Bengal, nor, given the suggested 'bonds of alliance', sovereign enough, Jinnah rejected the offer.

He also asked Gandhi to agree that Muslims and Hindus were separate 'nations', that voting in any plebiscites should be restricted to Muslims, and that separation should precede, not follow, the end of British rule, propositions unacceptable to Gandhi.

'Let us call in a third party or parties to guide or even arbitrate between us,' Gandhi suggested on 22 September. Jinnah did not agree, and he also turned down Gandhi's wish to present his scheme to the League's executive committee.

Azad in prison thought that the exercise had only increased Jinnah's prestige. Yet the talks had also exposed the problematic nature of the League leader's demands. For in his talks with Gandhi, Jinnah had insisted that Pakistan would include West Bengal and East Punjab, large areas where Muslims constituted a minority.

But if Hindu-majority areas could belong to Pakistan, why shouldn't Muslim-majority areas remain in India? And if non-Muslims in Muslim-majority areas were not entitled to a vote, what rights could Muslims demand in Hindu-majority areas?

From these unsuccessful talks, Gandhi took away an intriguing question about Jinnah. Born in Karachi but owning property in Bombay, Delhi and Simla, and enjoying a large practice in Bombay and Delhi, concerned with Muslims in Muslim-majority areas but also with Muslims in Hindu-majority areas, how deeply did this Jinnah desire a separated Pakistan?

■

On 15 March 1946, Churchill's successor as prime minister, Clement Attlee, told the House of Commons that Britain had decided to leave India. Later in the month, three ministers of the British Cabinet—secretary of state for India Pethick-Lawrence, India expert Stafford Cripps, and A. V. Alexander, a trade union leader who had become first lord of the admiralty—arrived in India to try to resolve the Pakistan demand and also to convert the viceroy's executive council into an interim national government.

Viceroy Wavell joined as the fourth member of Britain's negotiating team, which conferred with Indian politicians during all of April and May and most of June in New Delhi and Simla.

Never before had three Cabinet ministers from Britain spent three summer months together in India. The main discussion was on a scheme thought up by Cripps of a three-tiered India where provinces would form the bottom tier, two groups of provinces (one in the northwest and another in the east) the middle tier, and a union the top tier. If they agreed to combine, the two groups in the middle, inclusive of all of Punjab, Sindh, Balochistan, the NWFP, all of Bengal, and Assam, would constitute Large Pakistan, although the Cabinet Mission, as it was called, did not use that phrase.

Jinnah said he could accept the scheme if the union was nominal and the groups could later secede from it. The Congress said it could accept the scheme if the union was real and if provinces like the NWFP, where a Congress ministry had again been elected earlier in the year, and Assam, where Muslims constituted a minority, could stay out of the groups.

The Cabinet Mission did not speak plainly. It did not tell the Congress and the League that a real union *and* a large Pakistan space went together. If the Congress wanted League support for an undivided India, it *had to* accommodate a large 'Pakistan area'. If the League wanted Congress backing for a *large* Pakistan area, the latter would have to exist *within* an Indian Union.

Instead, the Mission spoke in two voices. On 16 May it produced an ambiguous plan which both the Congress and the League 'accepted' with opposing interpretations, enabling the Mission to claim 'success'.

This 16 May text said in Paragraph 15 that provinces 'should be free to' form groups and in Paragraph 19 that they 'shall' do so. Later, Cripps would candidly tell the House of Commons that the wording was kept 'purposely vague' to enable both sides to join the 16 May scheme.

The document also said that union and group constitutions could be reconsidered ten years after being framed, a provision welcomed by the League as a door to secession. In short, while the League in effect pronounced the *union* in the 16 May scheme to be optional, the Congress claimed that the middle tier of the *groups* was not essential.

On 24 May, an aide to the Mission and a future British MP, Woodrow Wyatt, advised Jinnah that though Pakistan had not been conceded he could accept 16 May 'as the first step on the road to Pakistan'. On 6 June the League formally 'accepted' the 16 May plan, while adding that 'complete sovereign Pakistan' remained 'its unalterable objective' and claiming that 'the foundation of Pakistan' was 'inherent' in what it described as the plan's 'compulsory grouping' and in the implied 'right of secession'.

Explanations and assurances of the opposite kind were offered to the Congress, enabling it to 'accept' the 16 May scheme even as it insisted that the phrase 'should be free to' ruled out compulsory grouping in the first place.

'Accepting' these heavily qualified 'acceptances' from the Congress and the League, Wavell installed, in the autumn of 1946, an interim government in New Delhi, formally still called the viceroy's executive council, composed mostly of Congress and League representatives. Nehru, who had succeeded Azad as Congress president, joined as member for external affairs and vice-chairman, as did Patel (as home member), but Jinnah stayed out, asking Liaqat Ali Khan, who became member for finance, to lead the League group.

This interim government of India was thus established in a climate of deep mistrust, with the Congress and the League persisting in their clashing interpretations of the Cabinet Mission's longer-term plan for provinces, groups and the union.

Troubled by the Mission's doublespeak, Gandhi wrote to Cripps on the night of 24 June that he proposed 'to advise the Working Committee not to accept the long-term proposition', adding, 'I must not act against my instinct'.

At the Working Committee meeting the next morning, where Gandhi asked his secretary, Pyarelal, to read out his note to Cripps, members responded with uncomfortable silence.

Gandhi said to them: 'I admit defeat. You are not bound to act upon my [advice]... I shall now leave with your permission.' After a hush, Azad, who was presiding, asked the others, 'What do you desire? Is there any need to detain Bapu any longer?' The silence continued, and Gandhi got up and left.

Close colleagues and lieutenants of his for thirty years, Nehru, Patel, Azad, Rajagopalachari, Prasad and company, seemed more interested in immediate power than in clarity about the future.

Even so, Gandhi's response was to back the Working Committee before the Empire, the Muslim League, and the world. To him, the colleagues rejecting him were India's best. They represented the Congress mind. They were the future. He would support them despite the rebuff, despite his knowledge that a game of doublespeak was being played on all sides, and despite his sense, to which he gave expression, that violence was in the air.

When the AICC met in Bombay on 7 July to pronounce on the Working Committee's acceptance of the Cabinet Mission Plan, with Nehru taking over from Azad as the head, a recently released Jayaprakash Narayan argued that the plan was a trap. Gandhi admitted that 'the darkness' he had felt about it had not lifted. Yet he added,

> The Working Committee [members] are your faithful and tried servants. You should not lightly reject their resolution.

The AICC ratified the decision, by 204 to 51.

■

The Congress and the League continued to accuse each other of doublespeak. Charging that the Congress had been taken into the interim government despite its 'dishonest' interpretation of the Mission's plan, Jinnah called for 'direct action' on 16 August 1946.

The result was major violence in Calcutta (where numerous Hindu deaths on 16 August were quickly outnumbered by Muslim deaths), followed by killings in eastern Bengal in September (with hundreds of Hindus killed, raped and forcibly converted), killings in Bihar in October and November (when 7,000 or more Muslims perished), and violence in Garhmukteshwar in UP in November, when nearly a thousand Muslims were killed.

Three months later, on 20 February, came a declaration in London by His Majesty's Government that the British would leave India within sixteen months and in any case not later than June 1948. Prime Minister Attlee said that the departing Empire would hand over 'to some form of Central Government or in some areas to the existing provincial governments' or 'in such other way as may seem most reasonable'.

Attlee added that Wavell would be replaced as viceroy by Lord Louis Mountbatten, a forty-six-year-old admiral related to King George VI.

Informed in advance of the coming announcement, the Empire's guardians in India had advised against it. The Punjab governor, Evan Jenkins, predicted that it would cause 'all parties' in Punjab to try to 'seize as much power as they can—if necessary by force'. Wavell, the viceroy who was being ordered out, thought that a deadline would drain the morale of British officers and soldiers in India, an opinion shared by General Auchinleck, the commander-in-chief.

However, the Empire in retreat ignored the advice of colony-based officers. In Punjab, where 'the existing provincial government' was in the hands of the Punjab Unionist Party's Khizr Hayat, and Khizr's Hindu and Sikh allies, the thought of all of Punjab going under that government triggered an immediate agitation by the province's majority Muslims.

Women took to the streets. Students blocked trains. Kinsmen deserted Khizr. Caving, he resigned on the night of 3 March, and the Muslim League tried to form a successor government.

This did not happen, and Governor's Rule was imposed instead, but violence erupted. Between 5 and 8 March, two thousand or more Sikhs and Hindus were killed in and around the cities of Rawalpindi, Attock and Multan in West Punjab.

On 8 March, pressed by Punjab's Sikh and Hindu leaders and shaken by the violence, the Congress Working Committee, meeting in New Delhi, asked for 'a division of the Punjab into two Provinces, so that the predominantly Muslim part may be separated from the predominantly non-Muslim part'.

With this resolution, the Congress was conceding Pakistan, while also insisting that East Punjab would stay out of it. Soon a division of Bengal was also demanded. When the League asked for a division of India, the Congress had said no. Now the Congress was asking for partition, with Jinnah continuing to hold that all of Bengal and Punjab belonged to Pakistan.

When the Congress resolution was passed, Gandhi was in distant Bihar, striving to restore peace there, even as he had earlier strived in Bengal. Learning of the resolution from newspapers, he sent questioning letters to Nehru and Patel.

He was not giving up. Reflecting on Punjab's armed bands, on Jinnah's opposition to the division of Punjab and Bengal and on the Congress's dislike of India's division, Gandhi felt that if the Congress accepted a Jinnah-led ministry in New Delhi to replace the feuding and non-functional interim government, polarization could be reversed, and peace and unity preserved.

Travelling to Delhi, Gandhi presented his proposal to Congress leaders and the newly-arrived viceroy, Lord Mountbatten, in the first days of April.

Let Jinnah (Gandhi told the Viceroy) head an interim government of his choice, comprising League members alone or a broader one. Secondly, unless an impartial umpire, e.g. the viceroy, were to rule that a League measure was against the national interest, the Congress, which had a majority in the Central Assembly, would back the League government.

Thirdly, Punjab's private bands should be disbanded. Finally, if Jinnah and the League were not willing, under these terms, to form a cohesive government, Nehru and the Congress should be given the same opportunity.

Gandhi thought that the League leader, who had dismissed Gandhi's separation scheme in 1944, would be open to his latest proposal. However, the young admiral taking over in New Delhi had not only determined that partition *was* the solution—a conclusion that Nehru and Patel too had reached—he had prepared a precise plan for partition.

Perturbed therefore by Gandhi's proposal, Mountbatten was shaken when Azad told him (on 2 April) that Gandhi's plan was 'perfectly feasible of being carried out'. As the Viceroy recorded:

> I told [Azad] straightaway of Gandhi's plan, of which he already
> knew from Gandhi that morning. He staggered me by saying
> that in his opinion it was perfectly feasible of being carried
> out, since Gandhi could unquestionably influence the whole of
> Congress to accept it and work it loyally. He further thought
> that there was a chance that I might get Jinnah to accept it,
> and he thought that such a plan would be the quickest way
> to stop bloodshed.

Would Jinnah agree to the proposal? Though never putting it to
the League leader, Mountbatten indirectly probed him on 9 April
by saying (not very honestly) that 'it was a daydream of mine to be
able to put the Central Government under the Prime Ministership
of Mr. Jinnah himself'. Thereafter, according to the Viceroy, Jinnah
'once more appealed' against 'a moth-eaten Pakistan'. However,
Mountbatten's record continues,

> [S]ome thirty-five minutes later, Mr. Jinnah, who had not
> referred previously to my personal remark about him, suddenly
> made a reference out of the blue to the fact that I had wanted
> him to be the Prime Minister. There is no doubt that it had
> greatly tickled his vanity, and that he had kept turning over
> the proposition in his mind. Mr. Gandhi's famous scheme may
> yet go through on the pure vanity of Mr. Jinnah!

Though promising Gandhi that he would examine the scheme and
privately telling his staff that 'it would not be very easy for Mr.
Jinnah to refuse Mr. Gandhi's offer' and that 'basically Mr. Gandhi's
objective was to retain the unity of India and basically he was right
in this', Mountbatten was in fact opposed to the scheme.

Thanks to skilful work put in by his staff, associates and himself,
the Viceroy's anxiety was removed. To strengthen the opposition
of Nehru and Patel to Gandhi's plan, the Viceroy, supported by
Jawaharlal's friend V. K. Krishna Menon (who had befriended

Mountbatten in London), worked on Nehru, while V. P. Menon (a talented member of the Viceroy's staff who enjoyed a close relationship with Patel) liaised with the home member. V. P. Menon also produced, on 5 April, a detailed note for the Viceroy entitled, 'Tactics to be adopted with Gandhi as regards his scheme'.

The upshot was that Gandhi's Congress colleagues firmly rejected his proposal, which therefore was never put to Jinnah. On 11 April, in a letter to Mountbatten, Gandhi admitted defeat:

> I had several short talks with Pandit Nehru, and an hour's talk with him alone, and then with several members of the Working Committee last night about the formula I had sketched before you, and which I had filled in for them with all the implications. I am sorry to say that I failed to carry any of them with me except [Ghaffar] Khan...
>
> I could not convince them of the correctness of my plan... Nor could they dislodge me from my position although I had not closed my mind... Thus I have to ask you to omit me from [further consultations].

A diary entry by Rajagopalachari (member of the interim government and a participant in the deliberations to which Gandhi referred) states that Gandhi's 'ill-conceived plan of solving the present difficulties' was 'objected to by everybody and scotched'.

Jinnah scholars in Pakistan have on the whole doubted that he would have agreed to Gandhi's proposal. However, Stanley Wolpert, Jinnah's American biographer, thought that Gandhi's plan 'might just have worked'. 'Surely', Wolpert wrote, 'this was a King Solomon solution'.

After admitting defeat, Gandhi left Delhi for Bihar. In the middle of June, when the All India Congress Committee met to ratify the partition to which Nehru, Patel and company had agreed, Gandhi told the AICC that he was acquiescing in it.

On 14 August, in Karachi, Jinnah was sworn in as Governor General of a Pakistan without East Punjab, West Bengal or Assam, and with Liaqat Ali as prime minister. In New Delhi the next day, Jawaharlal Nehru and Vallabhbhai Patel took over the government of a truncated but independent India as prime minister and deputy prime minister, respectively, with Mountbatten continuing as Governor General.

Earlier that morning, 15 August 1947, Gandhi had opened his eyes in a decaying Muslim-owned house in Beliaghata, a depressed Hindu-majority locality in Calcutta, where, once more, Gandhi strove to bring peace, for violence had broken out there.

The story of Gandhi's final phase—his intervention in Calcutta, his response to the upheaval and carnage in Punjab and Delhi, and the course on which he installed independent India before his assassination in January 1948—is told later in this book, in Chapter 7. Before that we will examine Gandhi's role in the questions of castes and inequalities in India, and take a closer look at his nonviolence.

CHAPTER 6

OF CASTE AND AMBEDKAR

Perhaps no one was personally closer to Gandhi than his English friend
Charlie Andrews, whom he first met in South Africa in 1912. In
August 1942, when Andrews was no more, Gandhi would say, 'There
were no secrets between us. We exchanged our hearts every day'.

In the summer of 1933, Andrews urged Gandhi to concentrate
on the removal of untouchability 'for the whole remainder of your
life, without turning to the right or the left'. Recalling that Gandhi
had 'again and again' said that with untouchability Indians were 'not
fit' for Swaraj, Andrews asked his friend not to try 'to serve two
masters'. This is how Gandhi replied:

> Now for your important argument about untouchability. But
> there is this initial flaw about it. My life is one indivisible whole.
> It is not built after the compartmental system—satyagraha, civil
> resistance, untouchability, Hindu–Muslim unity... are indivisible
> parts of a whole...
>
> You will find at one time in my life an emphasis on one
> thing, at another time on other. But that is just like a pianist,
> now emphasizing one note and now [an]other. But they are
> all related to one another.

Adding that 'full and final removal of untouchability' was 'utterly
impossible without Swaraj', Gandhi signed off as 'Mohan', for
Andrews, addressed by Gandhi as Charlie, was one of the very few
who called Gandhi by his first name.

Even as America fought first for independence and next for preserving its union before it could tackle slavery, Gandhi thought that India needed independence for overcoming the evils of caste arrogance and untouchability, but it had to be an independence that clearly recognized the evils.

Gandhi, as we saw, sounded the untouchability note early in his life, starting with boyhood clashes with his mother over playing with the 'untouchable' youngster Uka, who came to the Gandhis' Rajkot home to clean it.

In South Africa in the 1890s, Gandhi hired Indians of 'untouchable' background in his law office, lodged some of them in his Durban home, and had that well-known fight in 1897 with Kastur over her reluctance to cheerfully remove an 'untouchable' lodger's chamber pot, a fight that also revealed, as Gandhi confessed, his domineering nature.

At the end of 1908, when Indians arrested for defying South African laws were packed inside jails in groups, and a high-caste satyagrahi refused to sleep next to an 'untouchable', Gandhi expressed outrage. 'This was humiliating', Gandhi wrote in his journal, *Indian Opinion*, adding:

> Thanks to these hypocritical distinctions of high and low and to the fear of subsequent caste tyranny, we have...embraced falsehood... I wish that Indians who join this movement also resort to satyagraha against their caste and their family and against evil wherever they find it.

The note became even stronger when Gandhi returned to India in 1915 and started a centre in Ahmedabad. Opposition to untouchability was one of the *vows* taken by those joining the centre, which Gandhi called an ashram.

When Dudabhai Dafda, an 'untouchable', was admitted to it with his wife, several objected, including a crucial colleague and relative, Maganlal Gandhi, and Maganlal's wife, Santok, as also Gandhi's wife Kastur.

To a friend in southern India, Gandhi wrote that he had told
Kasturba that if she was unable to live with the 'untouchable' couple,
'she could leave me and we should part good friends'. Kasturba
yielded and stayed, but not Maganlal's wife.

Santok fasted in opposition to the admission of Dudabhai and
his wife, Gandhi fasted back, Santok and Maganlal packed their bags,
said goodbye, and left. Later they returned, having, as Gandhi would
say, 'washed their hearts clean of untouchability'.

When they tried to take water from a well next door, Dudabhai
and other members of the ashram were chased off by neighbours,
and money ceased to come in. Gandhi was thinking of moving the
ashram into an 'untouchable' settlement when a young industrialist
then in his twenties, Ambalal Sarabhai, quietly drove up, handed Rs
13,000 to Gandhi, and left.

The tide soon turned, and Dudabhai and his wife, both showing
forbearance, found increasing acceptance from neighbours, visitors
and ashramites.

In February 1916, Gandhi said in Madras: 'Every affliction that
we labour under in this sacred land is a fit and proper punishment
for this great and indelible crime that we are committing'.

At a meeting in Godhra in Gujarat in November 1917, where,
as a police agent noted, Hindus, Muslims and untouchables were
present, Gandhi declared that the higher castes would become 'fit for
Swaraj' only when they stopped thinking of the untouchables as low.

When the Non-cooperation Movement for Swaraj was launched
in 1920, the Congress, thanks to Gandhi's insistence, made the
abolition of untouchability a central political goal. Orthodoxy hit
back, picking in particular on a decision by Gujarat Vidyapith, a
university in Ahmedabad that Gandhi helped create, not to take
students from schools that excluded 'untouchables'.

A leading journal, Gujarati, alleged that Christians like Andrews
had influenced Gandhi's stand against untouchability, and Gandhi
was warned that 'the movement for Swaraj will end in smoke' if
'untouchables' were admitted to schools endorsed by the movement.

Gandhi answered that he would rather reject Swaraj than abandon the 'untouchables', but the threat to back the Empire also came from some leaders of the 'untouchables', who argued that salvation for their people was 'only possible through the British Government'.

In April 1921, Gandhi asked 'untouchables' in Ahmedabad to assert their self-respect and urged them to 'cease to accept leavings from plates' and to 'receive grain only—good sound grain, not rotten grain—and that too only if…courteously offered.' Gandhi added:

> I prayed…today: 'If I have to be reborn, I should be born an untouchable, so that I may share their sorrows, sufferings and the affronts levelled at them, in order that I may endeavour to free myself and them from that miserable condition.'

The 'I should be born an untouchable' sentence revealed, among other things, Gandhi's realism. He knew that in the end the 'untouchables' would accept the lead only of one of their own. Still, he would try to win them and, at the same time, shame the orthodox.

In his journal he wrote that cruelties to the 'untouchables' constituted 'an outrage grosser than that in the Punjab against which we have been protesting'. This was a reference to the Amritsar massacre. Repeating the thought at the Ahmedabad meeting, he added:

> What crimes for which we condemn the Government as Satanic have we not been guilty of towards our untouchable brethren?… We make them crawl on their bellies; we have made them rub their noses on the ground; with eyes red with rage, we push them out of railway compartments—what more than this has British rule done?

■

Despite these convictions, there were times between the mid-1920s and the mid-1930s when Gandhi professed to see virtue in an ideal caste system. He seems to have done this to retain caste Hindu backing, which he needed for Swaraj and also for Hindu-Muslim partnership.

While claiming that an ideal caste system would produce a perfect division of labour and preserve skills from generation to generation, Gandhi took care to clarify in the same breath that such a system was purely imaginary and never existed.

His fight against untouchability intensified in the 1920s and the 1930s, and his attack on the high and low notion was relentless. What was missing was an open denunciation of the caste system as such.

Moreover, Gandhi's 'defence' of this system was joined by occasional disapproval, in line with traditional practice, of inter-caste dining and inter-caste marriages. While pleasing caste Hindus, Gandhi's stance alienated radical foes of caste, of whom the Dalit leader, Bhimrao Ambedkar (1891-1956), a brilliant scholar and lawyer armed with advanced degrees from the US and Britain, was the most resolute.

Eight years after Gandhi's death, Nehru would tell a European journalist, Tibor Mende:

I asked [Gandhi] repeatedly: why don't you hit out at the caste system directly? He said, 'I am undermining it completely by tackling untouchability'.... [Gandhi's] genius lay in finding the weakest point of the enemy, the breaking of his front.

Realizing that he would unite pro-orthodox ranks if he started with an attack on caste, Gandhi chose to zero in on an evil none could defend. The strategy worked, but his seeming defence of caste did not sit well with reformers.

For some years in the 1920s, Ambedkar was an admirer of Gandhi. In 1927, when Ambedkar led a satyagraha, as he called it, for Dalit access to a water tank in Mahad in western Maharashtra, Gandhi's photograph was displayed at the satyagrahis' rally. When they surged forward to the tank and drank from its water, they were attacked with sticks and clubs by infuriated bands of the orthodox.

Ambedkar wisely asked his people not to hit back. Gandhi justified the satyagraha in his journal and praised the Dalits' 'exemplary self-restraint' under Ambedkar's leadership. He also urged 'every Hindu opposed to untouchability' to publicly defend the courageous Dalits of Mahad 'even at the risk of getting his head broken'.

For a while Gandhi thought Ambedkar was a radical Brahmin fighting untouchability but he realized his mistake in August 1931, when the two met for the first time.

Within weeks of this encounter, the two took part in a London conference called by the Empire to discuss India's political and constitutional future. Before leaving India for this conference, Gandhi frankly admitted that Swaraj could make Dalits 'worse off' because it would give the upper castes political power on top of their social and economic strength:

> If we come into power with the stain of untouchability unaffected, I am positive that the 'untouchables' would be worse off under that 'Swaraj' than they are now, for the simple reason that our weaknesses and our failings would then be buttressed by the accession of power.

Since the Swaraj goal could not be abandoned, the solution, as Gandhi saw it, was to attack untouchability while asking for Swaraj.

A few months earlier in 1931, the Congress had met in Karachi, with Vallabhbhai Patel in the chair, and passed a 'fundamental rights' resolution. Drafted mainly by Gandhi and Nehru, this resolution pledged that a free India would abolish untouchability and provide equal rights to all, irrespective of caste, sex or creed. Nineteen years later, the pledge was enshrined in free India's Constitution, of which Ambedkar would be the principal architect.

At the 1931 London conference, however, a sixty-two-year-old Gandhi and a forty-year-old Ambedkar clashed over separate versus joint electorates. If the Empire could provide separate electorates and reserved seats for Muslims, Sikhs and India's Europeans, why not reserved Dalit seats and a separate Dalit electorate, ensuring that only Dalits voted for or against Dalit candidates? Gandhi answered the argument with a counter-question:

Sikhs may remain as such in perpetuity, so may [Muslims], so may Europeans. Will untouchables remain untouchables in perpetuity?

Indian reformers, Gandhi added, were fighting untouchability. Separating Dalits from the rest of Hindu society would hurt the slender bridge of overdue justice that was being created. There was another reality to which Gandhi confessed in a meeting at Friends House, the Quaker centre in Euston:

The 'untouchables' are in the hands of superior classes. They can suppress them completely and wreak vengeance upon the 'untouchables' who are at their mercy. I may be opening out my shame to you. But....how can I invite utter destruction for them?

We should mark that in London, Gandhi lived amidst the poorer-off in Kingsley Hall in the East End as the guest of the Quaker activist, Muriel Lester.

Gandhi acknowledged Ambedkar's commitment and abilities but also claimed that if it came to a choice, India's Dalits would pick him rather than Ambedkar as their representative, a claim truer in 1931 than in 2017.

Ambedkar's demand for a separate electorate was backed in London by many delegates, most of them nominated by the Empire. Before the conference ended, London signalled that a separate electorate for Dalits was likely. Shocking many, Gandhi declared before leaving London that he might fast unto death against it.

■

The animated dispute over separate electorates was proceeding alongside the fight for Swaraj. Because of that fight, the Empire arrested Gandhi in January 1932, within days of his return to India, and sent him to Yeravada Jail in Pune. There he was in September 1932 when the Empire announced (from London) a separate Dalit electorate, whereupon, from prison, Gandhi announced a fast of indefinite duration.

Directed at the separate Dalit electorate, the fast prodded the caste Hindu conscience and produced a quick result.

Meeting in Bombay, India's most influential caste Hindu leaders resolved, in line with the Karachi Resolution of March 1931, that 'one of the earliest Acts of the Swaraj Parliament' would be to assure to the 'untouchables' equal access to 'public wells, public schools, public roads and all other public institutions'.

There were other reactions to Gandhi's fast. Hindu temples closed for centuries to the 'untouchables' opened their doors. Brahmins invited Dalits to meals in their homes. The Empire, on its part, opened the doors of Yeravada prison, and Ambedkar and other Dalit leaders went inside to confer with Gandhi.

A settlement was reached. Under it, Gandhi not only agreed to reserved seats or quotas for Dalits in legislatures, he also said that Dalits should have seats in proportion to their population. In the Empire's scheme, only half of that number had been provided.

On his part, Ambedkar and his colleagues agreed to give up the demand for a separate electorate. On 24 September 1932, what became known as the Poona Pact was signed. A cable went to London, where His Majesty's Government accepted the joint proposal sent from one of its imperial prisons, and Gandhi broke his fast.

Seventeen years later, the essence of this pact was incorporated into free India's Constitution. Every subsequent Indian election in the eighty-two years since the pact—whether nationwide or in a state, town or village—has been conducted on its basis, with reserved seats for Dalits but without a separate electorate.

Gandhi claimed during the fast that 'an increasing army of reformers' would resist the 'social, civic and political persecution of the Depressed Classes'. The issue was of 'transcendental value, far surpassing Swaraj', he added.

Expressing what he called his 'Hindu gratitude' to 'Dr Ambedkar' and also to 'Rao Bahadur Srinivasan and Rao Bahadur M. C. Rajah',

Dalit leaders who had conferred with him in Yeravada, Gandhi added:

> They could have taken up an uncompromising and defiant attitude by way of punishment to the so-called caste Hindus for the sins of generations.
>
> If they had done so, I at least could not have resented their attitude and my death would have been but a trifling price exacted for the tortures that the outcastes of Hinduism have been going through for unknown generations. But they chose a nobler path and have thus shown that they have followed the precept of forgiveness enjoined by all religions. Let me hope that the caste Hindus will prove themselves worthy of this forgiveness.

To caste Hindus, he conveyed a warning:

> The political part of [the settlement]…occupies but a small space in the vast field of reform that has to be tackled by caste Hindus during the coming days, namely, the complete removal of social and religious disabilities under which a large part of the Hindu population has been groaning.
>
> I should be guilty of a breach of trust if I did not warn fellow reformers and caste Hindus in general that the breaking of the fast carried with it a sure promise of a resumption of it if this reform is not relentlessly pursued and achieved within a measurable period.

Wondering whether caste Hindu change was going to be deep enough, or wide enough, or lasting, Gandhi wrote to Andrews on 30 September 1932:

> I did expect a mighty response from the orthodox, but I was unprepared for the sudden manifestation that took place. But I shall not be deceived. It remains to be seen whether the temples opened remain open and the various other things done persist.

■

Was reform 'relentlessly pursued and achieved within a measurable period'? Much was done, but much more remained undone. Did Gandhi then start another fast unto death? He did not, though in May 1933 he again fasted for twenty-one days over untouchability.

Pointing to some of modern India's ugly realities, including over caste, some have asserted that Gandhi was a hypocrite and a secret foe of the Dalits. The record, however, shows that his fight against heavy odds was quite remarkable, even if success was only partial.

Shortly after signing the pact, Ambedkar said he had been 'surprised, immensely surprised' to find 'so much in common' between Gandhi and himself. 'If you devoted yourself entirely to the welfare of the Depressed Classes,' Ambedkar said to Gandhi, 'you would become our hero'. This, as we know, is what Andrews too said. But Gandhi's fingers would not stay away from the piano keys of Swaraj and Hindu-Muslim friendship.

In a book that Ambedkar wrote in 1945, thirteen years after the fast and the Poona Pact, he sharply attacked the fast that had led to the pact but not the pact's terms, which he claimed as a victory. He wrote, 'When the fast failed and Mr. Gandhi was obliged to sign a pact—called the Poona Pact—which conceded the political demands of the Untouchables, he took his revenge by letting the Congress employ foul electioneering tactics to make their political rights of no avail'.

In this 1945 text, Ambedkar also said that while 'the Untouchables were sad' because of the concessions he had made, '[T]he caste Hindus very definitely disliked [the Pact], although they had not the courage to reject it'.

■

We should mark the Empire's peculiar relationship with Gandhi in the 1930s. It not only allowed the fasting prisoner to change a major policy, it also allowed him to edit from jail a journal called *Harijan,* through which he hoped to continue his campaign against untouchability.

In the new journal's issue of 11 February 1933 Gandhi explained the choice of the word 'Harijan'. He recalled that an 'untouchable' reader of his earlier journal *Navajivan* (which the Raj had banned) had suggested using the expression 'Harijan'—God's person—for an 'untouchable'. Narsi Mehta, the author of 'Vaishnava Jana', had employed the phrase centuries earlier, the man had added.

Today almost everyone in India uses the term Dalit, which means downtrodden. Until about the 1980s, for about a half century that is, 'Harijan' was a widely-used term, but strong opposition by Ambedkar's followers and a number of Dalit leaders pushed it almost completely out of circulation. Condescension and worse was read into 'Harijan', yet many, including some Dalits, continue to employ the word.

When the journal *Harijan* started, Gandhi wrote that God was above all the protector of the helpless. Since none were more helpless than the 'untouchables', the word 'Harijan' for them seemed appropriate. When caste Hindus realized their folly and repented, they too, said Gandhi, would be entitled to be called Harijans.

Asking caste Hindus to recognize that many among them, whatever they might claim, 'despised' Dalits, Gandhi wrote:

> If to relegate a body of people to distant locations, to regard their touch, approach or sight as pollution, to throw at them the leavings of one's food, to deny them the use of public roads and institutions, even the use of public temples, is not to despise them, I do not know what the word 'despise' means.

His portrayal of Dalit hardship, presented in November 1932, was stark:

> Socially they are lepers. Economically they are worse than slaves. Religiously they are denied entrance to places we miscall 'houses of God'. They are denied the use, on the same terms as the caste men, of public roads, public hospitals, public wells, public taps, public parks and the like, and in some cases their approach within a measured distance is a social crime, [or]... their very sight is an offence.

They are relegated for their residence to the worst quarters of cities or villages where they practically get no social services. Caste Hindu lawyers and doctors will not serve them... Brahmins will not officiate at their religious functions. The wonder is that they are at all able to eke out an existence or that they still remain within the Hindu fold. They are too downtrodden to rise in revolt against their suppressors.

Orthodox hostility to Gandhi's stand produced two attempts on his life in 1934—one in Jasidih in Bihar and the other in Poona. Certain, however, that orthodoxy was losing ground, Gandhi wrote to Nehru in February 1933:

The fight against sanatanists is becoming more and more interesting if also increasingly difficult... The abuses they are hurling at me are wonderfully refreshing. I am all that is bad and corrupt on this earth. But the storm will subside...[I]t is the death dance of the moth round a lamp.

■

Though he had signed the Poona Pact, in the following year Ambedkar turned down Gandhi's request for 'a message' for the journal *Harijan*. Instead he sent a 'statement' where he said that nothing short of 'the destruction of the caste system' would finish untouchability. Outcastes existed, he said, because there were castes. He also signalled a readiness to leave the Hindu fold. Responded Gandhi:

If this doctrine of utmost superiority and utmost inferiority, descending from father to son for eternity, is an integral part of Hinduism...then I no more want to belong to it than does Dr. Ambedkar. But...there is no superiority or inferiority in the Hinduism of my conception.

I invite Dr. Ambedkar to shed his bitterness and anger and try to learn the beauties of the faith of his forefathers. Let him not curse Hinduism without making an unbiased study of it, and if it fails to sustain him in his hour of need, by all means let him forsake it.

•

When a huge earthquake destroyed towns and villages in north Bihar in January 1934, Gandhi suggested that the event was 'a divine chastisement' for 'the great sin' committed by the so-called higher castes against Harijans 'from century to century'.

Criticizing Gandhi's 'superstitious' argument, his friend Tagore, the Nobel laureate, commented that the logic 'far better suits the psychology of [Gandhi's orthodox] opponents than his own', and that the orthodox were likely to 'hold [Gandhi] and his followers responsible for the visitation of Divine anger'.

But Gandhi was not deterred. Again using the earthquake to drive home the iniquity of untouchability, he said on 24 January 1934,

[W]hilst we have yet breathing time, let us get rid of the distinctions of high and low, purify our hearts, and be ready to face our Maker when an earthquake or some natural calamity or death in the ordinary course overtakes us.

Large numbers of caste Hindus were part of the immense crowds Gandhi drew while journeying across India to raise funds for the anti-untouchability effort. There were moments when Gandhi thought, in his words of March 1934, that 'untouchability has become weak and limp'.

But in India's villages attacks on Dalits did not cease. In October 1935, shortly after reports of atrocities in Ahmedabad district's Kavitha village, Ambedkar announced that though born a Hindu he did not intend to die one. Gandhi offered an immediate comment:

I can understand the anger of a high-souled and highly educated person like Dr Ambedkar over the atrocities as were committed in Kavitha and other villages. But religion is not like a house or a cloak which can be changed at will...

However, Gandhi now decided to criticize the caste system directly. On 16 November 1935, he said of the caste system, 'The sooner public opinion abolishes it, the better.' The *Harijan* article in which he wrote this was headlined, in large type, CASTE HAS TO GO.

The next year, 1936, Ambedkar published his famous lecture, *Annihilation of Caste,* after a reformist group in Lahore, reading an advance text of the lecture they had invited Ambedkar to deliver, cancelled the event. Reviewing *Annihilation of Caste,* Gandhi criticized the cancellation, reiterated his rejection of caste, which he deemed 'harmful both to spiritual and national growth', and did what he had thus far hesitated to do: he publicly affirmed his acceptance of inter-dining and inter-marriage.

Claiming however that the Indian term 'varna' was different from caste, Gandhi tried to defend 'varna' by saying that the hereditary occupations for which 'varna' stood could ensure harmony and economy. At the same time Gandhi clarified that restoring a pure varna system was like 'an ant trying to lift a bag of sugar' or 'Dame Parkington pushing back the Atlantic with a mop'. He was admitting that the varna system was a fantasy.

Ambedkar easily picked holes in Gandhi's theoretical defence of varna, which had, however, soothed Gandhi's caste Hindu constituency.

∎

At the end of March 1938, while he, Kasturba, Mahadev and others were in Orissa, Gandhi learnt that Kasturba, Mahadev's wife, Durga, and a woman relative of Durga's had gone inside Puri's famed Jagannath Temple, from which Dalits were barred. He was shocked, and also troubled, for 'the whole of Puri' was evidently talking about Kasturba's visit inside the temple. The stationmaster asked a member of the Gandhi team, 'Did Kasturba really enter the temple?'

Chastised by Gandhi, the women wept. Kasturba said she was wrong to have gone inside. Gandhi's strongest rebuke, however, was reserved for Desai. He should have advised the women not to go in, Gandhi told him. Mahadev's fifteen-year-old son, Narayan, was praised by Gandhi. Though accompanying the women, Narayan had refused to go inside. The rebukes and the praise were recorded in Gandhi's journal.

From the late 1930s, Gandhi blessed marriages between Dalits and non-Dalits in his ashram and in circles close to him.

Between 1937 and 1939, Congress governments in the provinces, each of them containing a Dalit minister, strove to improve the Dalits' situation. In Madras Presidency, a new law made discrimination against Dalits in jobs, wells, public conveniences, roads, schools and colleges an offence. Another law enabled Dalits to enter several of the south's great temples for the first time in centuries.

In elections to these provincial legislatures in early 1937, as also in a central legislature election held in 1934, almost all Dalit seats were won by Dalit members of the Congress. In Bombay Presidency, to which Ambedkar belonged, his party won a fair number of seats, but everywhere else the Congress's hold over Dalit seats was overwhelming.

When in December 1939 the Congress ministries resigned because of the Empire's refusal to promise India's independence at the end of the War, Ambedkar joined Jinnah in celebrating their departure. In 1941, after the League's Lahore Resolution, Ambedkar published a significant text, *Thoughts on Pakistan,* in which he seemed to see reason in the Pakistan demand.

Then when the Congress went into rebellion and launched Quit India, the Empire inducted Ambedkar into the viceroy's executive council. Ambedkar became Member for Labour in the executive council of an Empire that had put Gandhi, Nehru, Patel, Azad and thousands of popular figures in prison.

It was while he was a Member of the Viceroy's Council that Ambedkar wrote his 1945 text, *What Congress and Gandhi Have Done to the Untouchables,* in which he attacked Gandhi for his 1932 fast while maintaining that the Poona Pact was a victory for Dalits. By this time, the War had ended, Gandhi and company were out of prison, and fresh negotiations and elections were around the corner. Ambedkar hoped to improve his party's performance. However, elections in the winter of 1945–46 confirmed that the Congress commanded the bulk of the Indian electorate, including a majority of Dalit voters. It won an even larger proportion of Dalit seats than it had in 1937.

•

As independence neared, Gandhi felt freer to be openly radical. On 1 August 1946, a year before independence, he wrote to Vallabhbhai Patel:

> Who are the people who beat up Harijans, murder them, prevent them from using wells, drive them out of schools and refuse them entry into their homes? They are Congressmen. Aren't they? It is very necessary to have a clear picture of this.

Three months after writing this letter, Gandhi found himself in Noakhali in eastern Bengal, where communal violence had flared up. In January and February 1947, he and his companions, walking from village to village, halted overnight in forty-seven different East Bengali homes, where their hosts, many of them Dalits, included washermen, fishermen, cobblers and weavers.

In Noakhali, Gandhi told caste Hindu women that if they continued to disown the 'untouchables', more sorrow would be in store. Hindu village women were given the radical advice noted in a previous chapter:

> Invite a Harijan every day to dine with you. Or at least ask the Harijan to touch the food or the water before you consume it. Do penance for your sins.

On 24 April 1947, less than four months before independence, Gandhi said publicly in Patna that for some time he had 'made it a rule... to be present or give his blessings' only for a wedding between a Dalit and a non-Dalit.

•

An Ambedkar-Congress rapprochement was under way by 1947. One of Ambedkar's biographers, C. B. Khairmode, has described a conversation in December 1946 between Ambedkar and Gandhi's British friend, Muriel Lester, who had hosted Gandhi during the London conference of 1931, when Gandhi and Ambedkar clashed.

Lester informed Ambedkar that 'Gandhi was keen that the Congress should include Ambedkar in the central Cabinet and use his learning and leadership…' According to Khairmode, Ambedkar gave an encouraging response, which Lester conveyed to Gandhi, who then asked Nehru and Patel to invite Ambedkar to join free India's first Cabinet.

Gandhi's wooing of Ambedkar during the winter of 1946-47 is corroborated by a public statement he made in East Bengal on 3 February 1947. Regretting the Muslim League's boycott of the Constituent Assembly, Gandhi added: 'Dr. Ambedkar was good enough to attend the Assembly'.

At this point partition was not yet accepted, the Congress and the League were jockeying for influence, and it was Jinnah in fact who had first brought Ambedkar into the Constituent Assembly. This was done via the Bengal legislature, where the League held many seats. After the Empire offended Jinnah by inviting the Congress into an interim government, the League boycotted the Constituent Assembly, but Ambedkar did not, thereby eliciting Gandhi's praise.

Two years earlier, during the 1944 Gandhi-Jinnah talks in Bombay, both leaders had cited Ambedkar's book, *Thoughts on Pakistan*. In Gandhi's assessment, Ambedkar's talents were exceptional.

Another Ambedkar associate, Roshanlal Shastri, has written that he was present in Delhi when Ambedkar received a phone call from Rajkumari Amrit Kaur, one of Gandhi's close colleagues, requesting Ambedkar, on Gandhi's behalf, to join Nehru and Patel in government.

Thus an Englishwoman and an Indian Christian lady from Punjab were among Gandhi's emissaries to Ambedkar.

On 26 July 1947, three weeks before independence, Gandhi spoke, in a conversation with Dr Syed Mahmud of Bihar, of the folly of rejecting capable individuals merely because they had worked for the Empire:

> They have not become our enemies because they served the British Government... Please remember that they are at heart patriots... If we seek the advice of such...persons, they will show their genius.

Before the month of July ended, Nehru and Patel extended the invitation to Ambedkar. Accepting it, Ambedkar became India's law minister, chaired the committee that drafted the Constitution, and piloted the Constitution Bill into law.

■

The invitation and its acceptance were statesmanlike moves. As a result of Ambedkar's induction into Constitution-making, a brilliant and passionate human being, who happened also to be an Indian and a Dalit, piloted a Constitution assuring equal rights to all in a society that for centuries had called people like him inferior, and untouchable, and an elected Constituent Assembly, where a large majority were caste Hindus, welcomed and adopted such a Constitution.

In the light of earlier history, this was a notable achievement, and one that compensated to some extent for the tragedy and price of Partition.

When, two months after Gandhi's death, Ambedkar married Sharada Kabir, a Brahmin doctor, (his first wife, Ramabai, had died in 1935), Vallabhbhai Patel wrote to him, 'I am sure if Bapu were alive he would have given you his blessings.' Ambedkar replied, 'I agree that Bapu, if he had been alive, would have blessed it'.

They had their differences and clashes. In 1951, three-and-a-half years after Gandhi's death, Ambedkar resumed his opposition to the Congress. In 1956, shortly before he died, Ambedkar renounced Hinduism and accepted Buddhism, along with hundreds of thousands of followers.

Still, history shows that Gandhi and Ambedkar had much in

common. Both understood the inevitability of conflict between sections of a diverse and at times sharply divided people. Both agreed, however, that struggle had to be resolute, fearless, passionate but also peaceful, for killing damaged a struggle's goal.

For Ambedkar, and also for Gandhi, Dalit solidarity, Dalit education and the Dalit vote were weapons far superior to the lathi or the gun; when used by a vulnerable Dalit, the latter only played into the hands of the better armed enemy.

Both realized that the culmination of a struggle for justice was usually negotiation and a settlement rather than surrender by the foe and complete triumph for one's side. Despite harsh experiences, both knew that the adversary in a struggle, the Other, was a human being too, and that justice seldom endured without reconciliation.

•

In June 1947, two months before independence, Gandhi proposed a strong symbolic move: appointing a Dalit woman or man as free India's first president.

The proposal was sparked off by the death, at the end of May, of Chakrayya, a talented young Andhra Dalit who had been at Gandhi's Sevagram ashram from its inception. Gandhi had nursed high hopes for Chakrayya. 'I feel like crying over his death,' he said, 'but I cannot cry. For whom should I cry and for whom should I refrain from crying?' On 2 June he said at his prayer meeting:

> [T]he time is fast approaching when India will have to elect
> the first President of the Republic. I would have proposed the
> name of Chakrayya, had he been alive.

On 6 June he repeated the thought in a conversation with Rajendra Prasad, suggesting at the same time that a few prominent leaders should stay out of the government:

> If all the leaders join the Cabinet, it will be very difficult
> to maintain contact with the people at large…That is why I

suggested even in my prayer speech that a Harijan like Chakrayya or a Harijan girl should be made the nation's first President and Jawaharlal should become the Prime Minister… [S]imilar arrangements [can be] made in the provinces too…

Three weeks later he returned to the idea in a public utterance:

27 June: [I]f I have my way, the President of the Indian Republic will be a chaste and brave Bhangi girl. If an English girl of seventeen could become the British Queen and later even Empress of India, there is no reason why a Bhangi girl of robust love of her people and unimpeachable integrity of character should not become the first President of the Indian Republic…

By electing a Harijan girl to that office we shall…show to the world that in India there is no one high and no one low… She should be chaste as Sita and her eyes should radiate light… We shall all salute her and set a new example before the world.

If such a girl of my dreams becomes President, I shall be her servant and I shall not expect from the Government even my upkeep. I shall make Jawaharlal, Sardar Patel and Rajendra Babu her ministers and therefore her servants.

Gandhi's radical suggestion of a Dalit head of state was turned down. Nehru, Patel and company wished to retain Mountbatten as Governor General. They thought the subcontinent's princely states would be more likely to choose India over Pakistan if the King's cousin continued as Governor General.

Gandhi agreed to Mountbatten staying on, but repeated that he wanted an 'untouchable' to head the Indian state before long.

In his 14 June speech to the AICC in which he conveyed his acquiescence to partition, Gandhi said that just as, in the Ramayana, the tragedy of Rama's exile was followed by something wonderful, from partition's pain even good might come, provided the so-called 'untouchables', the other so-called lower castes, the Adivasis, Muslims,

Parsis and Jews (all these groups were separately named) were treated with respect in the India that remained.

On 23 November, after independence, Gandhi spoke publicly in Delhi of the Dalits' continuing hardship in southeastern Punjab, the Haryana of today:

> It is a matter of shame for us that there are... Jats and perhaps Ahirs too [who feel] that the Harijans [are] their slaves... They may be given water and food but they can get nothing by right... We feel that we can even intimidate a judge if we are brought before him... The result is that the Harijans are ruined.

In the afternoon of 30 January 1948, when Congress leaders from East Punjab called on him at Birla House in New Delhi, Gandhi again remembered the piano's sad keys that had always compelled him. 'How are the Harijans?' he asked the higher-caste leaders.

He would be killed two hours later. The man shooting into Gandhi's unprotected chest and his co-conspirators were highest-caste Hindus.

CHAPTER 7

AHIMSA AND GANDHI

Blessed in Hinduism, Buddhism and Jainism, the ancient doctrine of ahimsa had been reduced to rules of diet, but in Gandhi's hands it became an explosive yet constructive force.

An elderly Russian I met in Moscow in 1994 told me of the impact on Russians in 1922, more than seven decades ago, that is, of Gandhi's abrupt suspension of an India-wide non-cooperation campaign. Gandhi had called it off because an angry Indian crowd brutally killed twenty-two Indian policemen employed by the British Empire.

This response by Gandhi, the Russian told me, was contrasted in the Moscow of 1922 with Lenin's defence of the murder of some of 'the class enemy' who lay ill in a hospital. 'These things happen in a revolution,' Lenin had evidently said.

Gandhi hoped to go beyond nonviolence to the removal of hatred. Louis Fischer, the American writer who met Gandhi several times in the 1940s, said that Gandhi wished 'to liberate India in order to liberate England from India'. 'He had no animus,' Fischer added. 'He was incapable of hatred.'

In this chapter we will look at Gandhi's journey to nonviolence or ahimsa, and also at what became Gandhi's ahimsa.

From his autobiography, we know that in Rajkot the adolescent Mohan was *not* against violence. Arguing that Indians strengthened with meat would physically drive away their British rulers, Mohan's brother Karsan, and the brother's friend Mehtab, enlisted him for secret meat-eating assignations.

As a young boy, Mohan heard of ahimsa from his Gujarati Bania relatives and from Jain monks visiting his home, but this ahimsa applied chiefly to diet. However, Mohan also responded to a stanza in his schoolbook that spelt out ahimsa in a deeper sense. The Gujarati poet Shamal Bhatt had said (in translation):

> For a bowl of water give a goodly meal;
> For a kindly greeting bow thou down with zeal;
> For a simple penny pay thou back with gold;
> If thy life be rescued, life do not withhold...
> And return with gladness good for evil done.

From Rajkot, an eighteen-year-old Mohandas travelled all the way to London in 1888. During three years in England as a student of law, he crossed, as he puts it, 'the Sahara of atheism'. The call for forgiveness and non-retaliation in the Sermon on the Mount, which he read while in England, 'went (in his words) straight to his heart'.

But there was no rejection of militancy. In an article for a London magazine *The Vegetarian* (28 February 1891), Gandhi proudly wrote of 'an Indian shepherd' as 'a finely built man of Herculean constitution' who 'with his thick strong cudgel would be a match for any ordinary European with a sword'.

Returning to India in 1891, Mohandas began an immediate friendship with Rajchandra, the Jain poet, thinker and jeweller who was three years older than him, which lasted until Rajchandra's early death in 1901.

A scholar of Jainism, Hinduism and religion in general, Rajchandra reminded Gandhi of the ancient Hindu maxim, 'Ahimsa Paramo Dharma', or ahimsa is the highest duty, which was also a central Jain and Buddhist tenet.

Long and deep conversations took place between Rajchandra and Gandhi, but these seemed confined to an individual's moral and spiritual goals and did not enter into the rightness or wrongness of violence on behalf of an ill-treated people.

Soon after these conversations with Rajchandra in Bombay, Gandhi experienced in Rajkot (in late 1892 or early 1893) the 'first great shock' of his life, as he calls it in the autobiography. He was forcibly ejected from the office of the Resident, Charles Ollivant, when he had gone there to intercede on behalf of his brother.

A proud barrister who was also a proud descendant of ministers in Kathiawar, Gandhi seethed with rage. Perhaps, as Ollivant had claimed, it was an impropriety to recall chance London meetings to help a brother. Still, being physically ejected felt intolerable.

Gandhi informed Ollivant in writing that he would initiate legal action for assault. However, India's pre-eminent lawyer of the day, Pherozeshah Mehta, who happened to be in Rajkot at the time, warned young Gandhi not to invite ruin by proceeding against a senior Raj official. Gandhi pocketed the humiliation.

Though the anger against Ollivant cooled with time, Gandhi may have entertained violent thoughts for a while. This is suggested by a remark that Gandhi made much later, in 1924:

As a coward, which I was for years, I harboured violence. I began
to prize non-violence only when I began to shed cowardice.

Persuaded by Mehta, he had failed to implement his warning to Ollivant. To Gandhi, this was cowardice. Having swallowed the humiliation, he was assailed by violent thoughts. We do not know precisely what the thoughts were.

Gandhi was capable of imagining and describing violent scenes. Thus in 1925 he wrote: 'I have had in my life many an opportunity of shooting down my opponents and earning the crown of martyrdom, but I had not the heart to shoot them. For I did not want them to shoot me.'

And in 1931 he said: 'Having flung aside the sword, there is nothing except the cup of love which I can offer to those who oppose me.'

We know that he never acted upon his violent thoughts. We can imagine that he was repelled by their appearance, a natural reaction in one receptive to the Shamal Bhat verse, the Sermon on the Mount, the ancient Hindu maxim on ahimsa, and the ideas of self-control he had discussed with Rajchandra.

Yet it appears that violent thoughts continued to prey on his mind. It was only after he developed a nonviolent way of fighting, a process that evolved in South Africa during the thirteen years between 1893 and 1906, that the temptation of violence left his system.

The Ollivant episode was a major reason (Gandhi tells us) why he had seized the South African opening offered by the Porbandar-born merchant, Abdullah Sheth. Gandhi needed to get out of Ollivant's orbit as quickly as possible.

From the moment of his arrival in South Africa, the twenty-three-year-old Gandhi kept his eyes wide open against any mistreatment of Indians. This now is a vigilant Mohandas, in fact one ready to fight, but also a wary one.

Never forgetting that in that brief interview before the ejection Ollivant had claimed the moral high ground, young Gandhi wanted to be sure that in any future encounter with the Empire, he would occupy that superior space. 'Never again,' he told himself, would he be caught in a 'false', i.e. morally weak position, he informs us in the autobiography.

Within days of landing in Durban on South Africa's east coast, Gandhi made that well-known journey to Pretoria that all (including Gandhi) agree altered his life. Though holding a first-class ticket, he was tossed out of the train in Pietermaritzburg, his only offence being that he was not white.

It was wintertime in the southern hemisphere. Rejecting a temptation to return to India, he decided, in the station's cold waiting-room, to stay in South Africa and fight. After a decent enough train ride the following morning to the town of Charleston, he was badly beaten up on the journey's next leg, which was by stage-coach to Standerton, for refusing to sit 'on a piece of dirty sack-cloth' spread out on the footboard, away from all the other passengers, which the conductor had ordered him to occupy.

Though pushed and thrashed, Gandhi hung on to the rails of the coach-box. Eventually the conductor ceased beating him. In Johannesburg, where there was an overnight halt, hotels barred their doors to him, but an Indian merchant offered accommodation. The next morning it was with difficulty that Gandhi managed to secure a first-class seat on the train from Johannesburg to Pretoria.

Resisting degrading treatment and standing his ground, Gandhi had regained the self-respect snatched from him by the Ollivant episode. Also, and this too was significant for Gandhi, he no longer had to choose between two life-goals, one spiritual and the other political. A fight to uphold the equal worth of all human souls, whether the body around the soul had a white, brown, black or yellow skin, would be a spiritual as well as a political exercise.

During his months in Pretoria in 1893-94, Gandhi moved closer to ahimsa, thanks largely to what he read. Tolstoy book, *The Kingdom of God is Within You,* was the strongest influence. Gandhi found it more appealing than the mainline Christian tracts that friends in Pretoria were asking him to read.

Pretoria's young Gandhi had plenty of time. The case for which he had been hired was yet to pick up steam. He walked, read, and reflected, went to churches and joined numerous lunches where participants, including Gandhi, went down on their knees to pray for light: he was the only non-white among them.

In October 1893, he journeyed a long distance from Pretoria to attend a large Christian convention in Wellington, forty miles from Cape Town.

Yet it was the Tolstoy book that uniquely gripped him, offering Jesus's Sermon on the Mount, from which Tolstoy underlined five commandments: love your enemies, and do not hate, lust, hoard or kill. Gandhi felt 'overwhelmed,' he would say, by the 'independent thinking, profound morality and truthfulness' in Tolstoy's presentation.

Another significant influence on the young Gandhi was his reading of books on India's 1857-59 Revolt, which had begun with the mutiny of the sepoys. As a schoolboy in Rajkot he had heard of the Revolt, which ended only ten years before Gandhi's birth. In old age Gandhi would describe the climate prevailing in Rajkot and much of India during his boyhood, saying:

> The Sepoy War was quelled by means of superior force. Outwardly things quieted down but the hatred against an imposed rule went deep underground.

In the summer of 1891, just before a twenty-one-year-old Gandhi left England to return to India, a friendly British jurist called Frederick Pincott asked him to read up recent history. In particular, said Pincott, Gandhi should study the volumes about the 1857 Revolt by Kaye and Malleson. Two-and-a-half years later, in Pretoria, Gandhi acted on the advice.

There is no record of his immediate reactions to the six volumes, yet we have to be impressed by the number of times the later Gandhi referred to the Revolt. In *Hind Swaraj*, written in 1909, he says more than once that a true satyagrahi should be ready to be blown from a cannon's mouth, which is how many rebels met their death in 1857.

On 24 July 1947, three weeks before Independence-cum-Partition, he expressed the fear—soon to be tragically realized—that India was moving towards a carnage even worse than that of 1857:

> [W]e are nurturing attitudes that will result in war and if this drift is not stopped we shall find ourselves in a conflict much more sanguinary than the Mutiny of 1857. India then did not have enough awakening and the mutiny was confined only to the sepoys. All that we did was to cut down Englishmen. In the end the British army overcame the mutineers.
>
> God forbid that the present strife should ever assume such dimensions... I shall appeal to you not to prepare for warfare.

His study of 1857 had suggested to Gandhi that violence was folly. We may infer, too, that the link that the future Gandhi always made between fear and violence was connected to his study of 1857, when people on both sides feared they would be killed if they did not kill.

Though Tolstoy and the study of 1857 did not produce an allegiance right away to ahimsa, Gandhi's commitment to South Africa's Indians grew. In 1894, he organized the Indians of Natal and played the chief role in starting the Natal Indian Congress.

In January 1897, when he brought his family from India to South Africa, a white mob assaulted him on the streets of Durban. Narrowly escaping death, Gandhi decided, in the interest of good relations between Indians and whites, not to proceed against the assaulters in a court of law. But he did not talk of ahimsa.

Two years later, at the start of the Boer War (a clash between the British and the Afrikaaners, who were South Africa's dominant white groups), Gandhi led hundreds of Indians to the battlefield as ambulance workers on the British side as we saw earlier. Refusal to aid the British at that critical juncture, Gandhi reckoned, would invite fresh hostility towards Indians and demands for expulsion.

His life was changing. Simplicity became a goal, and he returned gifts he and Kasturba had received for serving the community. Since South Africa's Indians included Hindus, Muslims, Christians, Sikhs and Parsis, Gandhi looked for opportunities to strengthen inter-communal links. Indignities that he and all Indians faced in South Africa made him think of the indignities that India's 'untouchables' received from 'higher' castes.

He learnt an important truth or two also from his wife Kasturba, after she shamed him into seeing his domineering side when (in that well-known story) he tried to force her, in Durban in the late 1890s, to follow his rules for looking after an 'untouchable' house mate.

In 1902-03, a thirty-three-year-old Gandhi studied the Bhagavad Gita in depth. He had first encountered it in an English translation when studying in London. Now he immersed himself in the Gita and memorized it. Two truths from it he retained for life were, firstly, that his concern had to be about his actions, about what he should do, not about the fruits of his actions; and, secondly, that the world and everything in it belonged to God.

Also reading John Ruskin's *Unto This Last* at this time, Gandhi embraced the goal of social equality and told himself that a barber's work had the same value as a lawyer's.

When poor Indians living in a Johannesburg ghetto called Brickfields faced a plague epidemic, Gandhi led a successful effort to save lives. In 1903, he launched the journal *Indian Opinion* and in 1904 the Phoenix settlement near Durban, the first of Gandhi's ashrams.

In 1905, when Russia and Japan fought a war which the Asian power won, Gandhi commented several times on it in *Indian Opinion*, without mentioning violence or nonviolence.

His joy in the triumph of the Asian country was unconcealed. 'So far and wide have the roots of Japanese victory spread,' he wrote, 'that we cannot now visualize all the fruit it will put forth. The people of the East seem to be waking up from their lethargy'.

Now, however, he was on the eve of perhaps his greatest transformative experience, his four weeks in June-July 1906 as a stretcher-bearer and paramedic for the British colony of Natal which was trying to suppress a Zulu rebellion.

We have already looked, in Chapter 2, at that experience and at the birth, in consequence, of satyagraha.

■

I will not relate that story again. Instead let me offer a few short observations about Gandhi's nonviolence. One, the personal resolutions he made in Zululand for poverty and chastity were related to his keenness to face the world from a moral high ground.

Two, Gandhi's close reading of Henry David Thoreau's 'classic' essay, as Gandhi called it, on civil disobedience seems to have occurred some months *after* the meeting of 11 September 1906, when the Transvaal's Indians decided on their nonviolent disobedience. A year after that meeting, Gandhi extensively quoted Thoreau in *Indian Opinion*.

Calling Thoreau 'one of the greatest and most moral men America has produced', and lauding his opposition to slavery, Gandhi also said, 'Both his example and writings are at present exactly applicable to the Indians in the Transvaal'.

Gandhi seemed to find validation in Thoreau for the response that the Zululand experience and Transvaal's new Asiatic law had evoked from him.

Three, we should mark that all the episodes on Gandhi's journey to ahimsa occurred in multi-racial, multi-cultural settings. This was true of the Ollivant incident, of Gandhi's readings of the Gita, the Bible, and Tolstoy (all taking place far from India), and of the 1906 Zululand experience.

When, in November 1907, *Indian Opinion* invited essays on civil disobedience and announced prizes, it asked essay writers to absorb the writings of Tolstoy and Thoreau and the story of Socrates and to provide 'Biblical and other religious authorities' for their views.

The 1857 Revolt that also influenced him was again the story of more than one race.

We know, too, that Gandhi's ahimsa was not confined to the India-West encounter. Relations within the Indian world in South Africa, whether between Hindus and Muslims, caste Hindus and 'untouchables', males and females, or the rich and the poor, were also involved in Gandhi's ahimsa.

Four, in *Hind Swaraj*, written in November 1909, Gandhi theorized the satyagraha that he and his associates had practised in the Transvaal and presented nonviolent struggle, involving peasants and elites, as a strategy for India's freedom.

Five, this manifesto was evoked by a fascination for violence that Gandhi noticed in some Indians in South Africa and also among young Indians studying in England, whom he met on visits in 1906 and 1909. *Hind Swaraj* presented a strategic alternative to violence.

Six, a key argument for nonviolence that *Hind Swaraj* spelt out rested on human fallibility. Since human beliefs were not error-proof, killing for a belief could never be justified. As Gandhi wrote:

No man can claim to be absolutely in the right, or that a
particular thing is wrong, because he thinks so.

Seven, Gandhi was stirred by satyagraha's ability to empower the
weak and the crippled. As *Hind Swaraj* put it, 'Even a man weak
in body is capable of offering this resistance. One man can offer it
just as well as millions. Both men and women can indulge in [it].'

Violence, on the other hand, endangered the weak. In later years
(after returning to India), Gandhi would elaborate this point, declaring:

> We cannot win Swaraj for our famishing millions, for our
> deaf and dumb, for our lame and crippled, by the way of the
> sword... If the practice of seeking justice through murders is
> established amongst us, we shall start murdering one another for
> what we believe to be justice. In a land of crores of destitutes
> and crippled persons, this will be a terrifying situation.

Eight, in the biggest of South Africa's Gandhi-led struggles, the
Great March (1913) in Natal in which thousands of Indian workers
protested against a tax on their stay in South Africa, a vital role was
played by women.

Finally, we may note that when in 1915 Gandhi returned to
his motherland and started his first Indian ashram—which in his
case was a training centre for moral, social and political change—a
pledge of ahimsa was the very first of eleven *vows* that those joining
had to take. Truth, rejection of untouchability, fearlessness, and equal
respect for all religions were among the other vows.

■

So was Gandhi's ahimsa a way of struggle or a way of life? What
we have seen shows that for Gandhi ahimsa came intertwined with
struggle. The intertwining was so close and tight that ahimsa and
struggle seemed to become one thing. Ahimsa and satyagraha became
synonymous.

Ahimsa after Gandhi is thus very different from the ahimsa of which he heard in boyhood. What Indian tradition had reduced to a rule of diet emerged from Gandhi's hands as a weapon—a universal weapon—to fight oppression, not just alien rule, but also national evils like untouchability and Hindu-Muslim discord and indifference to suffering.

It became a way of life as well. The weapon of ahimsa fused with the element in Gandhi that had leapt up, when he was in his teens, on encountering the Shamal Bhat verse and the Sermon on the Mount. Gandhi insisted that there could be no ahimsa if compassion, forgiveness and equality were absent. A lesson in compassion was part also of Gandhi's Zululand experience, when he saw what bullets and lashes do to a human body.

Three years after that experience, when Gandhi was in England to educate its leaders and public on what Indians in South Africa were facing, he was asked to speak at London's Emerson Club. Saying that South Africa's 'grim prisons' where he and the other Indian satyagrahis had found themselves were the gateways to the 'garden of God' where the 'flowers of self-restraint and gentleness' grew 'beneath the feet of those who accept but refuse to impose suffering', Gandhi added these eloquent sentences:

War demoralizes those who are trained for it. It brutalizes men of naturally gentle character. It outrages every beautiful canon of morality. Its path of glory is foul with the passions of lust, and red with the blood of murder. This is not the pathway to our goal.

But if ahimsa meant compassion, and putting aside angers and hates, and identification with the poor, why didn't Gandhi use the old Christian word 'love'? Wasn't that positive expression better than the negative phrase ahimsa?

Gandhi liked the word 'love'. To underline what love could do—God's love for humans and human love for one another—Gandhi often resorted to Indian poets and saints, including Kabir, Nanak, Tulsidas, Tukaram, Mira and Narsi Mehta. On occasion he also invoked Paul of Tarsus.

In November 1917, after wondering what gift he should send to a favourite nephew, Maganlal, on what by the Hindu calendar was new year's day, Gandhi decided to send the lines on love in Paul's First Letter to the Corinthians, closing with, 'And now abide faith, hope, love, but the greatest of these is love.' Writing out the passage in Gujarati, Gandhi added:

> Read this. Chew the end. Digest it. Read the original in English, translate it into Hindi. Do all you can, strain your neck and eyes, but get a glimpse of this love or charity. Mira was stabbed with the dagger of love and she really felt the wound. If we too can get at this dagger, we can shake the world to its foundations.
>
> Though I feel I have something of this love, I am painfully conscious every moment how very shallow it still is. I weigh and find myself very much wanting... Only yesterday I saw I had no room in my heart for those who would not let me have my way.

Aware of Gandhi's response to 'love', several wanted to know why he preferred the expression 'nonviolence'. In 1936, he was asked by African American visitors—Howard and Sue Bailey Thurman and Edward and Phenola Carroll—why love as described by Paul was not enough for him. Answered Gandhi:

> In spite of the negative particle 'non', nonviolence is no negative power.... [W]e are surrounded in life by strife and bloodshed, life living upon life... But it is not through strife and violence but through nonviolence that man can fulfil his destiny... Ahimsa means love in the Pauline sense, and yet something more, although I know Paul's beautiful definition is good enough for all practical purposes.

Let us grasp what Gandhi was saying. Since the real world involved struggle, love and struggle had to go together. In other words, ahimsa was love plus satyagraha, a way of life plus a method of struggle.

As we have seen, it became a vow, and demanded compassion and the spirit of forgiveness from the vow taker. But Gandhi's ahimsa never abandoned the fight.

■

We must ask: how active was ahimsa, or love, in Gandhi's relations with his wife Kastur? In 1939, when Gandhi found himself in the NWFP, he narrated his personal experiences with Kastur, who was not present, to what we must assume was a mostly male audience.

Realizing that the gender question was relevant, Gandhi addressed it on 23 October 1939 in Hungoo, about twenty-five miles south of today's Pakistan-Afghanistan border:

> I used to be a tyrant at home… I used to let loose my anger at Kasturba. But she bore it all meekly and uncomplainingly. I had a notion that it was her duty to obey me, her lord and master, in everything.
>
> But her unresisting meekness opened my eyes and slowly it began to dawn upon me that I had no such prescriptive right over her. If I wanted her obedience, I had first to persuade her by patient argument. She thus became my teacher in nonviolence. And I dare say, I have not had a more loyal and faithful comrade in life.
>
> I literally used to make life a hell for her. Every other day I would change my residence, prescribe what dress she was to wear. She had been brought up in an orthodox family, where untouchability was observed. Muslims and untouchables used to frequent our house. I made her serve them all, regardless of her innate reluctance.
>
> But she never said 'no'. She was not educated in the usual sense of the term and was simple and unsophisticated. Her guileless simplicity conquered me. You all have wives, mothers and sisters at home. You can take the lesson of nonviolence from them.

In these sentences clearly aimed at macho Pashtuns, I find an unspoken admission from Gandhi that Kastur became his teacher in nonviolence not because she was meek and obedient, although he refers to her meekness; she became his teacher by frankly questioning him and confronting him with his domineering side. Despite the orthodoxy instilled into her, Kastur accepted his radical steps, but she did so as a partner, not as a subordinate.

Ahimsa after Gandhi must in any case include gender justice.

■

In respect of Gandhi's chastity vow, which he pondered from the year 1900 and took in 1906 in conjunction with his discovery of satyagraha, it is well known that Gandhi regarded perfect chastity—the brahmacharya of Hindu thought—as the source of power over forces threatening his goals. More than that, in the final phase of his life he conducted experiments, risky for himself and his women associates, to test his attainment of chastity.

These experiments seemed linked to a need for physical human contact, to bouts of shivering, and also to Gandhi's opinion that with perfect personal chastity he should be able to avert the looming partition and curb the killings that were spoiling his dream.

Without questioning the energy of chastity, it may be suggested that imperfect chastity may not have been the principal cause of partition and the related carnage. Other explanations, including some offered by Gandhi himself, are more satisfying.

■

We should mark that Gandhi did not lead or join a global anti-war or pacifist movement. After 1915, his field of action—his karmabhoomi—was India. If his ahimsa succeeded in winning Indian independence, if ahimsa built a fair, just and compassionate society in India—that would speak to the world.

Not only did Gandhi not join a global pacifist movement, in 1918 in Gujarat he tried to recruit soldiers to fight alongside the

British in World War I; in 1942 he said that, if freed, India would permit British and Allied troops to remain on its soil to bring World War II to a successful end; and in October 1947 he supported the dispatch of Indian soldiers to Kashmir.

Thus Gandhi's nonviolence was complex. We see this complexity in his reaction to a mutiny, eighteen months before independence, in the Royal Indian Navy. This mutiny of February 1946 was initiated by young naval ratings, Hindu and Muslim, who had been thrilled by exploits of the Indian National Army led by Subhas Bose, and in particular by the release, prompted by the Empire's political calculations, of three Indian National Army (INA) officers, a Hindu, a Muslim and a Sikh, earlier sentenced for life.

The naval mutineers were provoked by discrimination from some white officers and by the food issued to them. None of the large number of the navy's Indian officers joined their revolt, but many ratings did. For four days there was violence, chiefly in Bombay, with incidents also in the ports of Karachi, Vizag and Chittagong.

In Bombay, mill workers and many youth joined in rebellion, but when leaders of the mutiny met Vallabhbhai Patel and Jinnah, both Bombay-based, they were advised to end their mutiny.

On 23 February, fatigued organizers called off the mutiny, which along with related disturbances had resulted, over a four-day period, in 236 deaths and injuries to over a thousand.

Before learning that the mutiny had been called off, Gandhi commented that to compel 'a single person' to shout nationalist slogans was to a threat to 'the dumb millions of India'. The violence in the streets was 'unbecoming' and anti-poor, and the violence of the mutineers was thoughtless. 'For there is such a thing,' Gandhi added, 'as thoughtful violent action.'

Disagreeing with those who would 'rather unite Hindus and Muslims at the barricade than on the constitutional front', Gandhi said: 'Even in terms of violence, this is a misleading proposition… Fighters do not always live at the barricade. They are too wise to commit suicide. The barricade life has always to be followed by the constitutional. That front is not taboo forever.' He added:

> It is a matter of great relief that the ratings have listened to
> Sardar Patel's advice to surrender. They have not surrendered
> their honour... If [the mutiny] was for grievance, fancied or
> real, they should have waited for the guidance and intervention
> of political leaders of their choice.
>
> If they mutinied for the freedom of India, they were doubly
> wrong. They could not do so without a call from a prepared
> revolutionary party.

Thus a Gandhi disapproving of violence nonetheless examines
violence from the standpoint of effectiveness. He distinguishes
between thoughtless and thoughtful violence, between foolhardiness
and a mutiny that answered a 'call from a revolutionary party'.

∎

When violence among Indians accompanied Independence and
Partition, several of Gandhi's well-wishers, including Stuart Nelson
of Howard University, who was visiting India, and men like Swami
Sivananda of Rishikesh, asked him why years of teaching nonviolence
had not prevented killings. This is how Gandhi responded in July 1947,
before Punjab's great carnage occurred during August, September
and October of that year:

> 24 July 1947: Outwardly we followed truth and non-violence.
> But inwardly there was violence in us. We practised hypocrisy
> and as a result we have to suffer the pain of mutual strife. Even
> today we are nurturing attitudes that will result in war and if
> this drift is not stopped we shall find ourselves in a conflict
> much more sanguinary than the Mutiny of 1857.

The twin components of Gandhi's nonviolence, 'fear not' and
'hate not', were both difficult to practise, but the first found wider
acceptance than the second. Observing in his *Discovery of India* that
'the dominant impulse in India under British rule was of...pervasive,

oppressing, strangling fear', Jawaharlal Nehru added that, thanks to Gandhi,

> That black pall of fear was lifted from the people's shoulders, not wholly of course, but to an amazing degree... It was a psychological change, almost as if some expert in psycho-analytical methods had probed deep into the patient's past, found out the origins of his complexes, exposed them to his view, and thus rid him of that burden.

Hatred, however, proved more resistant than fear. Gandhi had warned his compatriots that hate was a master, not a slave, that it could not be confined to one channel, but he was not heeded.

On 16 June 1947, Gandhi pointed out that many in India had welcomed hate, saying:

> No one at the time (*during the battles for Swaraj*) showed us how to make an atom bomb. Had we known how to make it, we would have considered annihilating the English with it.

Because a violent alternative was not visible, Gandhi added, 'my advice was accepted'. Gandhi's analysis went against the pleasing belief that Indians generally had assented to his tough prescription, which was that while British rule had to be opposed, the English, the Scots, the Irish and the Welsh had to be accepted, even loved, as individuals.

A magnificent core of nonviolent satyagrahis indeed implemented the prescription. These included the carefully organized satyagrahis of Bardoli in Gujarat who brought the land tax down in 1928; the meticulously chosen Salt Marchers of 1930 who triggered an extraordinary nationwide rebellion; the gallant Khudai Khidmatagars of 1930, led by Abdul Ghaffar Khan, who neither retreated nor hit back when confronted with brute force; and the more than fifteen thousand disciplined participants of the nationwide individual civil disobedience of 1940-41.

But in its remarkable restraint, this core did not represent the mass attitude. Each time violence occurred during a Swaraj campaign, Gandhi would argue that unaddressed popular anger had abetted it. Although he frequently suspended a campaign because of violence, its resumption or a new campaign always followed at some point. For Gandhi could not indefinitely silence his or his people's urge for freedom.

To be asked to love the British people was too much for the great bulk of those who cheered and supported Gandhi-inspired satyagrahas, or took part in other revolts. Dislike for the British was common across India and also entirely natural.

The events of 1946 and 1947 showed, however, that it was only a short step from hating the British to hating Hindus or Muslims.

Indians had failed a tough test; they had not expelled their hate of the enemy they wished to oust, and now, in 1947, hate was flowing between Indian and Indian.

In the year 2017, we must acknowledge that hate continues to flow between Indian and Indian. It lies behind the blood that continues to flow in India and the subcontinent today.

When Gandhi said, 'We cannot love the Japanese and hate the English', he was speaking, as I see it, not just to the people of India, he was speaking to himself too. Anger and hatred made many attempts to fill his heart, which allowed entry at times to anger but never to hate. On 7 August 1942, on the eve of launching Quit India, he had asked for the removal of hatred against anyone, telling the large crowd gathered at Bombay's Gowalia Tank:

> If there is the slightest communal taint in your minds, keep off
> the struggle. We must [also] remove any hatred for the British
> from our hearts. At least in my heart there is no such hatred.
>
> At a time when I am about to launch the biggest fight
> in my life, there can be no hatred for the British in my heart.

Successfully schooling himself against hatred in his heart against the British, at times Gandhi retained feelings of anger. At these times, while liking and loving several British individuals, Gandhi did not see the British as *his* people.

Several factors contributed to the 1947 carnage. Some persistent Hindus, Muslims and Sikhs joined imperial divide-and-rule in deliberately stoking ill-will among Indians.

Where, putting his life at risk, Gandhi asked for calm and non-retaliation and fasted for peace, polarizers on both sides exaggerated the wrongs of the Other and glorified revenge. The message of friendship was passionately countered by a message of hostility.

Moreover, London's abrupt announcement on 20 February 1947 that the British would very soon leave all of India was not accompanied by any plan of who would replace them in Lahore, Calcutta or Delhi.

The result was an immediate and violent scramble for control, especially in Punjab, where Muslim, Sikh and Hindu leaders were unable to reach a compromise. The Jinnah-as-prime-minister idea that Gandhi came up with, which aimed specifically at the deteriorating situation in Punjab, was foiled by the Viceroy and the Congress leaders, who joined hands for the purpose.

As Punjabis were thrown into a collision course, the departing British abdicated responsibility. Returning home at the earliest became the dominant desire of most British soldiers, policemen and civilians.

As for the Raj's Indian police, crossing the border with their immediate families became the paramount urge of Muslim officers 'trapped' in Hindu-majority areas of Punjab and Bengal, and of Hindu and Sikh officers who found themselves in West Punjab or East Bengal.

Saving the bulk of the population was thus a task abandoned to the people, who in fact performed heroically. Courageously and quietly, a great many Punjabis saved fellow Punjabis of the Other religion, easily outnumbering those who killed fellow Punjabis. No underreported story can be greater or nobler than this one.

But in a climate that quickly became toxic, gangsters, criminals and drug and alcohol addicts became heroes. Greed for gold and houses played a part. On both sides of the new border, enraged refugees stoked passions. On both sides, former army men, including ex-INA men, provided expertise, leadership and weapons to attackers.

∎

In that climate of killings and mutual blame, Gandhi prescribed tough medicine. In December 1947, when someone showed Gandhi a couplet in an Urdu magazine asking for 'a new Ghaznavi to avenge the renovation of the Somnath Temple', he responded:

> It is painful to [read this]. [But] I cannot return evil for evil. [Hindus] must not remember the wrong that Ghaznavi did. Muslims must realize and admit the wrongs perpetrated under the Islamic rule.

Which was harder, we can ask: for Hindus not to dwell on the ancient wound from Ghaznavi, or for Muslims to admit who caused it? But can the wounds of a divided nation be healed without an honest and painful searching of hearts?

Eleven years after Gandhi was killed, on 22 March 1959, a man who knew something about wounds and was interested in healing, Martin Luther King Jr., spoke of Gandhi and also of Abraham Lincoln in a church in Montgomery:

> They killed him, this man who had galvanized 400 million [Indians] for independence... One of his own fellow Hindus felt that he was a little too favourable toward the Moslems... Here was a man of love falling at the hands of a man with hate... But the man who shot Gandhi only shot him into the hearts of humanity. Just as when Abraham Lincoln was shot—mark you for the same reason that Mahatma Gandhi was shot, that is, the attempt to heal the wounds of a divided nation—and Secretary Stanton said, 'Now [Lincoln] belongs to the ages.'

CHAPTER 8

THE LAST DAYS OF GANDHI

In this chapter we will attempt a journey across the final phase of Gandhi's life, a phase both sad and magnificent.

From the moment when, after three years of captivity, they were released in the 1945 summer, the Congress president at the time, Abul Kalam Azad, and the party's most popular leaders, Jawaharlal Nehru and Vallabhbhai Patel, nursed a desire for autonomy.

Gandhi, who had been released a year earlier, honoured this wish. The guide whose lead the Congress had sought for a quarter century was therefore marginalized for the last three years of his life.

Yet, during this period and especially in the final fifteen months, the conscience of an isolated Gandhi appeared to accomplish what may have been beyond the range even of the once unquestioned master of the Congress.

Between November 1946 and April 1947, when Nehru, Patel and Azad, as also their colleagues in the Congress leadership, Chakravarti Rajagopalachari and Rajendra Prasad, were part of an interim central government in New Delhi, the Mahatma—the Great Soul who had also been the Great Leader—served as *a simple relief worker* on the ground.

First he served in Noakhali in East Bengal, in fields moist with rain but also with the blood of Hindu victims, and then, from March 1947, in Bihar's baking countryside, where hearts were often as dry as the air, and where Muslims had been mercilessly attacked.

With Gandhi at different times were a handful of companions

and helpers, including his learned secretary Pyarelal, Pyarelal's sister Sushila, who was a doctor, the creative Satis Dasgupta, the scholarly Nirmal Bose, Gandhi's unflagging nineteen-year-old grand-niece, Manu, a grandnephew, Kanu Gandhi, and Kanu's Bengali wife, Abha.

As they reached out in Bengal and Bihar to those who had lost loved ones and also to those guilty of violence, Gandhi and his team risked life and ignored discomfort.

In overwhelmingly Muslim Noakhali, where hundreds of Hindus had been killed or forcibly converted, and many women raped, there was an uncorroborated but possibly true story of Gandhi being seized once by Muslim captors who set him free after he spoke to them.

At times, eight or so armed men from the Bengal Police, sent by the province's Muslim League Premier Suhrawardy, stood near Gandhi's team, which included Bibi Amtus Salam from Rajpura in East Punjab, yet it was chiefly by winning the people's goodwill that the team remained safe in Noakhali.

In January and February 1947, a seventy-six-year-old Gandhi and his tiny band walked on foot from place to place, halting for the night in *forty-seven* different villages. Their hosts included Maulvi Ibrahim in Fatehpur village (8 January) and Habibullah Patwari in Muraim (24 January).

Of the weavers, cobblers and fisherfolk who welcomed Gandhi and his party in their homes, Manu would note in her journal, 'They bathe us with love.' Rai Mohan Mali, a washerman, hosted Gandhi in village Dalta (23 January), and Gandhi lived in a weaver's home in Palla (27 January), where he said: 'A house full of love, such as this one, is superior to a palace where love does not reign.'

Every day Nirmal Bose gave lessons in Bengali to Gandhi, who would rise at or before four, read and write by the light of a kerosene lamp, spin his thread, conduct two prayer meetings, and promote, for the villagers' health, clean air, sunbaths, and mud packs for the forehead and abdomen. Sick children, Muslim and Hindu, drew 'Doctor' Gandhi's attention.

Much of his time was spent with Hindu women stricken with fear.

Bose noticed Gandhi's 'daily ministrations on behalf of love' and 'the extreme tenderness with which he regarded each individual' relating woes to him.

Recognizing that courage was needed more than consolation, Gandhi told bereaved Hindu women weeping before him in Jagatpur (10 January) that 'tears won't bring back the dead'. After the women left, he said to Manu that their faces would haunt him; all he could eat for dinner that evening was a lump of jaggery.

For days, Gandhi walked barefoot. Often the grass was soft, but when Manu saw cuts on his soles and protested, Gandhi replied: 'We don't go to our temples, mosques or churches with shoes on... We [are] tread[ing] on holy ground where people have lost their loved ones.'

Usually the walk would commence with a prayer-song, often 'Vaishnava Jana', about the marks of a true follower of Vishnu, or Tagore's poem, 'Ekla Chalo Re (Walk Alone)'. At times Gandhi asked Manu and others singing 'Vaishnava Jana' to rephrase the opening line and speak of 'the marks of a true Muslim'.

'The pitch of Gandhi's [own] voice was low, but the tune was correct,' a witness, D. G. Tendulkar, would recall.

On 31 January, Muslims in Navagram defended Gandhi's right to quote from the Quran, and in the village of Sadhurkhil, an influential Muslim, Salimulla Saheb, invited Gandhi (4 February) to hold prayers on his grounds, adding he would not mind if the Hindu verse about Rama was chanted to the clapping of hands.

'The Rama whom I adore,' Gandhi explained in Sadhurkhil, 'is God Himself", different from any historical Rama. 'He always was, is now and will be forever'.

When a maulvi said that Hindus willing to convert had at least saved their own lives, Gandhi was offended by the implied condoning of forced conversion. He told the maulvi: 'I am amazed that God has allowed someone with your views to become a scholar of Islam.'

Spinning, writing, treating the sick and, most of all, listening to the bereaved until early in the morning if necessary, Gandhi rarely slept more than four hours at night. That he remained fit was proof to him of God's kindness.

To Patel, home member in the interim government and anxious about Gandhi's security in the East Bengal hinterland, he wrote:

> There is the One…above all of us who will look after me, and He is able enough.

Manu cooked for Gandhi, washed his sore feet after walking barefoot and kept notes of his conversations and talks. But there were times in Noakhali when Gandhi did chores which hitherto aides had taken care of, like cooking and darning his clothes.

One evening that winter, when, using dry sticks for fuel, Manu heated water for Gandhi to wash his hands and face with before retiring, he was not pleased. 'Where people don't have twigs for baking their rotis,' he said, 'you want me to wash my face with warm water? I can understand heating water for bathing, but not for this.'

Someone who had run into Harilal deep in the south of India wrote to Gandhi that his fifty-eight-year-old son looked much older than his years. Seldom knowing how to reach his wandering son, on 22 January Gandhi sent Harilal a letter, via the person who had met him, inviting him to Noakhali. A month later he wrote again to his son, who however did not join the father.

With Mahadev Desai and Kasturba both gone—they had died during detention, along with Gandhi, in Pune, he in 1942 and she in 1944—his life was lonelier and harder than before. February was the month of Kasturba's death, which by the Hindu calendar had occurred on Shiv Ratri. In 1947, Shiv Ratri fell on 19 February. At 7.35 p.m. that evening, in the village of Birampur, Gandhi wrote in his diary: 'On this day, and exactly at this time, Ba quitted her mortal frame three years ago'.

Nirmal Bose, his companion and translator, thought that Gandhi's 'questioning attitude towards his own perfection' contributed to Gandhi's 'tenderness' which 'soothed' men and women and 'lifted them above their sorrows'.

Bose's goals in Noakhali included compiling quotations from Gandhi, who asked Bose not to be misled by sentences which showed Gandhi 'at his best' and 'presented a picture of his aspirations, not of his achievements'.

Bose answered this remark by quoting Tagore, who had said that a man should be judged 'by the best moments of his life, by his loftiest creations, rather than by the small-nesses of everyday life'. To this Gandhi's response was quite stunning:

> Yes, that is true of the Poet, for he has to bring down the light of the stars upon the earth. But for men like me, you have to measure them not by the moments of greatness in their lives, but by the amount of dust they collect on their feet in the course of life's journey.

Though full confession by perpetrators of violence was not forthcoming, there was remorse in several villages. In some, Muslim elders punished anyone committing fresh acts of harassment or looting against Hindu neighbours. Hindus who had fled returned. Chants and prayer songs were heard again. Conches were blown. Hindu women wore vermillion and bangles once more.

In Bhatialpur, Muslims pledged that they would risk their lives to protect Hindus and do their utmost to get looted properties and abducted women returned, and a temple idol was restored in the presence of Muslims who had earlier broken it.

Each dispersed to a different village, Gandhi's companions produced results. Amtus Salaam, who always slept with the Quran at her side, went on a fast in Sirandi when her call for a surrender of a sword used against Hindus was not heeded. While she fasted Gandhi wrote her a letter every day, sometimes twice daily. After twenty-five days, though the sword was not returned, Gandhi persuaded her to end her fast (20 January).

Eleven Muslims of Sirandi took the pledge, 'with God as witness,' that they would defend the right of Hindus to practise their faith and continue to search for the missing sword.

In the village of Jayag (29 January), the local zamindar, Barrister Hemanta Kumar Ghosh, donated his lands to Gandhi. Receiving a power of attorney from Gandhi, Satis Dasgupta's close colleague Charu Chowdhury established on Ghosh's lands a centre for Hindu-Muslim harmony and development which survives to this day.

•

When Gandhi arrived in Bihar in March 1947, its horrific November story was four months into the past, yet the province's Muslims, less than 13 per cent of the population, remained frightened. Around 7,000 of their number had been killed and nearly 10,000 homes destroyed. In most places, the state police had merely looked on.

Women and children were brutally killed, wells were stuffed with bodies, villages burnt down. Learning of the Bihar carnage on his way to Noakhali, Gandhi threatened a fast unto death if it did not cease, and Nehru, Patel and Prasad left Delhi to control the province. Violence ended but little was done for relief and rehabilitation.

Some in Bihar justified the November violence as a means of saving Hindus across India, including in Bihar, from attacks of the Noakhali kind. Told by Rajendra Prasad that many Biharis thought 'they had done well', Gandhi replied that 'it was to save them from that sin that he had come'.

Telling Bihar's premier Shri Krishna Sinha that killings in his province were 'like the Jallianwala massacre', Gandhi spoke with similar bluntness to officials, Congressmen and the public. To Congress workers in Bir he said (19 March):

> Is it or is it not a fact that quite a large number of Congressmen took part in the disturbances?[...] How many of the 132 members of your Committee were involved?[...]
>
> I wish to ask you, how could you live to see an old woman of 110 years being butchered before your eyes?[...] I will not rest nor let others rest. I [will] wander all over on foot and ask the skeletons [what] happened.

There was, he said, a way out for Bihar:

> The Hindus of Bihar have committed a grave sin. They will
> raise the head of Bihar...if they do honest reparations, greater
> in magnitude than their crimes. There is an English saying,
> 'Greater the sin, greater the saint'.

Abducted women, stolen goods and illegal arms should be returned,
Gandhi said, to the police or, he added, to him, Rajendra Prasad or
Syed Mahmud, a prominent Bihar leader. Or to Ghaffar Khan, who
had journeyed from the NWFP to assist in Bihar. The government
on its part should catch culprits and award due punishment.

Gandhi was in Bihar for most of March 1947, half of April and
about a third of May. Most of his nights in the province were spent
in Mahmud's home on the banks of the Ganga, but despite the heat
he managed to visit several villages and towns, at times on foot.

Within days of his arrival, Bihar's Hindus showed signs of remorse,
and Gandhi was given confessional letters, stolen goods and arms by
some November attackers. Pyarelal recorded a scene from the village
of Masaurhi, where fearful destruction had occurred:

> After the prayer address, Gandhiji stayed on to collect money
> for the Muslim relief fund. There was a stampede as everybody
> pushed forward to be the first to put his or her copper into
> the Mahatma's hands. As he bent forward with outstretched
> hands, he read in those faces, [trembling] with emotion, the
> unmistakable evidence that repentance had at last crept into
> their hearts.

■

In another chapter we found Gandhi opening his eyes on independence
day in a Muslim home called Hydari Manzil in Beliaghata, a poor
Hindu-majority district in Calcutta, and addressing, elsewhere in
the city, an immense gathering of Hindus and Muslims on Eid day,
which fell on 18 August.

Two days thereafter, however, the man at whose call India's prisons used to be filled and its streets emptied admitted that he was short of helpers. In a letter (20 August) to Jivanji Desai, manager in Ahmedabad of his journal *Harijan,* Gandhi said:

> I am very sorry to learn that you got the articles on Wednesday...
> I take the utmost care to see that you get all the material on Monday evening... I send the material by air-mail from Calcutta on Sunday. But...I have no paid employee... Do you send anybody to the airport on Mondays?

At the hour of India's freedom, the once all-commanding Gandhi seems helpless, almost stranded. The general who executed his strategies by the calendar and the map is now not only marginalized, he seems unsure. He plans to greet independence in Noakhali but Calcutta's insecurity detains him.

Though his itinerary has been blown away, Gandhi retains his calm, and during this Calcutta stay he writes out that famous answer to doubt:

> I will give you a talisman. Whenever you are in doubt, or when the self becomes too much with you, apply the following test. Recall the face of the poorest and the weakest man whom you may have seen, and ask yourself if the step you contemplate is going to be of any use to him?... Then you will find your doubts and yourself melting away.

An answer to uncertainty is what Gandhi himself needs at this moment. He still hopes to proceed to Noakhali, but Punjab's mounting violence calls him to that province. After consulting Nehru, Patel and Mountbatten, and presumably asking himself what would help India's weakest, Gandhi decides that accompanied by Suhrawardy, now no longer premier, he should go, as previously arranged, to Noakhali—to Pakistan, that is.

But a hostile demonstration at Hydari Manzil intervenes. At about 10 p.m. on the night of 31 August, angry Hindus smash the house's windows, doors and ceiling fans. Gandhi, Abha, Manu and Bisen come out to meet the demonstrators. Bricks and a lathi are thrown at Gandhi, at an unidentified Muslim present, and at Bisen, whom the crowd takes for a Muslim. Only the Muslim is hit.

Abha and Manu, 'two very brave girls', as Gandhi calls them, do not leave his side and hold on to him throughout the commotion. Instructing the Muslims in the house and two policemen present to remain calm, Gandhi folds his hands in the Hindu manner towards the demonstrators while firmly asking them to disperse, but they do so only after a police officer has arrived.

Going to sleep at 12.30 a.m., Gandhi is up again in three hours. He writes to Patel about the incident, refers also to Nehru, and says, 'I pin my hopes on you two'.

Soon he learns of killings elsewhere in Calcutta during the night and goes in the pre-dawn darkness to the affected areas, sees 'two dead bodies of very poor Muslims', and wonders about the city's peace. In the afternoon a telegram arrives from Nehru suggesting a visit to the Punjab 'as early as possible', whereupon Gandhi thinks *maybe* he should do so the next day, giving up Noakhali.

But after visitors bring more news of Calcutta's violence—around fifty were killed during the night of 31 August and the day of 1 September—Gandhi is clear. He would go neither to Noakhali nor to Punjab: he would stay put in Hydari Manzil and fast until peace returns. If Calcutta responds positively, he would go to Punjab with confidence.

The newly appointed governor of West Bengal is C. Rajagopalachari, living in the grand house built early in the nineteenth century for the Empire's Governor General in India. Running from that mansion to run-down Hydari Manzil, C. R. asks his old friend: 'Can you fast against *goondas*?' Gandhi replies that his fast can touch 'the hearts of those behind the *goondas*.'

Announced at 8.15 p.m. on 1 September, the fast makes an immediate impact. Violence dies down. Hindus and Muslims march jointly for peace. About 500 members of the Calcutta police force,

including a few Britons and Eurasians, start a twenty-four-hour
sympathy fast while remaining on duty. A professor would recall later:

> Some [university students]... gathered weapons from streets and
> homes at great personal risk and returned them to Gandhiji.
> Men would come back from their offices in the evening and
> find food prepared by their family ready for them; but soon it
> would be revealed that the women of the home had not eaten
> during the whole day... They could not understand how they
> could go on when Gandhiji was dying for [Calcutta's] crimes.

Ram Manohar Lohia, the Socialist leader, brought to Gandhi a group
of young Hindus who admitted complicity in violence and handed
over a small arsenal of arms, including a Sten gun. When members
of another gang turned up, asking for 'any penalty' and pleading,
'Only you should now end your fast,' Gandhi said they should go
'immediately among the Muslims and assure them full protection'.

At 6 p.m. on 4 September a deputation of Hindu Mahasabha,
Sikh and Muslim League leaders, headed by Suhrawardy, went up
to Gandhi's bedside in Hydari Manzil and asked for the fast to end.
Gandhi asked if they would risk their lives to prevent a recurrence
of killings. After withdrawing to another room, the leaders returned
with a pledge. Reminding them that 'above all, there is God, our
witness', Gandhi agreed to break his fast, which had lasted for seventy-
three hours.

On 1 September a young Hindu, Sachin Mitra, was killed in
Calcutta while defending Muslims, and on 3 September, another
young Hindu, Smritish Banerjee, lost his life guarding a peace
march. During the fast, 'processions of young women and girls of
both communities...walked across the city to Gandhi's lodging and
brought peace'.

The writer Martin Green would say later that Calcutta in
September 1947 showed the power of 'the saint, the martyr and
the virgin, [working] together'.

'Gandhiji has achieved many things,' Rajagopalachari observed, 'but in my considered opinion there has been nothing, not even independence, which is so truly wonderful as his victory over evil in Calcutta'.

Mercifully, the city would be spared large-scale Hindu-Muslim violence during the following seven decades.

■

On the night of 7 September, Gandhi took a train for Delhi to go on to Punjab. Because the Dalit colony where he had stayed on preceding Delhi visits was overcrowded with refugees, and Gandhi's safety could not be guaranteed there, home minister Patel, who met Gandhi at Shahdara station on the morning of 9 September, had arranged his stay at Birla House, belonging to Gandhi's friend from 1915, Ghanshyamdas Birla.

Unhappy not to be living in the Dalit settlement, Gandhi was more disturbed on learning what was happening in the capital. Hundreds had been killed in the preceding four days, 'localities like Karol Bagh, Sabzimandi and Paharganj were being emptied of Muslims', the city was under curfew, and people's rations were exhausted.

Within hours of arrival, Gandhi went to a camp near Humayun's Tomb where Muslims driven away from the princely states of Alwar and Bharatpur, part today of Rajasthan, had taken refuge, to the Jamia Millia, where many of Delhi's Muslims had huddled together, and to three camps filled with Hindu and Sikh refugees from West Punjab.

For a 'whole day long' he listened 'to the tale of woe that [was] Delhi'. Hindu and Sikh refugees told Gandhi that they had not forgotten his services to Punjab, but he 'had not undergone the hardships that they [had]…he had not lost [his] kith and kin…[he had] not been compelled to beg at every door'.

At the Jamia Milia, the educator and future Indian president Zakir Husain referred to his escape on a train a few days earlier: had a Sikh army captain and a Hindu railway official not intervened, Husain would have been killed. Gandhi heard, too, that Saifuddin

Kitchlew, for three decades a national-level leader of the Congress, was forced to flee from his Delhi home.

Gandhi's hosts at Birla House said the city was in such disarray that even they, belonging to one of India's richest families, had not been able to obtain fruits and vegetables.

Before night fell, Gandhi knew he would not proceed to Punjab. He would stay on in Delhi.

The next morning, when newspapers announced that Gandhi was staying on in the capital, a Sikh taxi driver told Brij Krishna, who had served as Gandhi's Delhi helper from 1920, when he quit St. Stephen's College to join the movement: 'If Gandhiji had waited some more days before coming to Delhi, all the Muslims here would have been eliminated.'

In the inflamed climate of September 1947, when refugees brought dreadful accounts from Pakistan, turning Delhi into a purely Hindu city was not a fantasy. Angry sections of the populace would have backed such a bid, and many civil and police officials would have connived at it.

Two days after Gandhi's arrival in Delhi, the US military attaché saw Muslim women and children being clubbed to death at Old Delhi's railway station even as soldiers looked on. A week later, an American diplomat said in a letter to Washington, '[T]here was no assurance that either police or Indian Army troops will interfere if [a Muslim] is attacked.'

Anti-Muslim elements in Delhi whispered that home minister Patel, staunchly Hindu in his heart, was secretly on their side. However, the home minister's hand was conscious of the law and also of Gandhi's presence. A day before Gandhi's arrival, Delhi's *Hindustan Times* published Patel's warning that partisan officials would be punished.

With Gandhi in Delhi, and home minister Patel plainly ready to do his bidding, the plan to expel or eliminate Delhi's Muslims was aborted.

Three days after reaching Delhi, Gandhi confronted the Rashtriya

Swayamsevak Sangh (RSS) chief, M. S. Golwalkar, with reports of the RSS's hand in the Delhi violence. Denying the allegations, Golwalkar said, in answer to a question from Gandhi, that the RSS did not stand for the killing of Muslims. Gandhi asked him to say so publicly. Golwalkar said Gandhi could quote him. This Gandhi did in his prayer talk that evening, but he told Golwalkar that the statement ought to come from him.

Four days later (16 September), at Gandhi's instance, a number of RSS activists called on him. He told them that zeal 'without purity of motive and true knowledge has been known to prove ruinous'.

Asked by an RSS member if Hinduism did not permit killing an evildoer, Gandhi answered: 'How can a sinner claim the right to judge or execute another sinner?' Only a properly constituted government was entitled to punish an evildoer.

∎

In September and thereafter, Gandhi's team and staff in Birla House included Abha, Manu, Brij Krishna, Bisen, Kalyanam, a stenographer, and, when they were in Delhi, Pyarelal and his sister Sushila. Most including Gandhi slept on mats on the floor in one room at the western end of the house. At three in the morning, Bisen roused everyone else, including Gandhi, but at times Gandhi performed the routine.

The room was also where, sitting on a thin mat covered with white khadi, Gandhi worked—writing, spinning, and receiving streams of callers—where he ate his meals, and where he and the others prayed before dawn each morning.

At five in the evening, Gandhi and his companions held open-air multifaith prayers at the southern end of the Birla House grounds. Anyone could join and also hear Gandhi's post-prayer remarks. Usually a few hundred did.

Delivered in simple Hindi (or Hindustani, as he preferred to call it), Gandhi's prayer-time talks were published by the newspapers and also relayed live over the national radio, which was in Patel's charge.

Gandhi prepared these talks with care, sometimes writing out, for the sake of the press, drafts in English. On 24 September he said:

> I have just a handful of bones in my body. But my heart belongs to me. So do your hearts belong to you...

If he could not improve the scene, said Gandhi, he would prefer being removed from it. Reading the sentence in Johannesburg, Sonja Schlesin, his secretary four decades earlier, sent Gandhi this letter for his seventy-eighth birthday.

> Far from losing your desire to live until you are 125, increasing knowledge of the world's loveless-ness and consequent misery should cause you rather to determine to live longer still... You said in a letter to me some time ago that everyone ought to wish to attain the age of 125, you can't go back on that.

We can picture Gandhi being touched. When an Indian wrote asking Gandhi to remember that he was 'the only instrument to further the divine purpose', *Harijan* (12 October) published the well-wisher's letter as well as Gandhi's response:

> I am not vain enough to think that the divine purpose can only be fulfilled through me... May it not be that a man purer, more courageous, more farseeing is wanted for the final purpose?

Seeing that Gandhi looked cheerful, an Indonesian visitor asked, early in November, for his secret. Replied Gandhi:

> I look after my health with care... Moreover, I consider no one as my enemy... I also resort to certain outward remedies. You see that even while guests such as you are visiting here I lie with a mud-pack on me. Do please forgive me my lack of manners.

Early in November, in a letter to one close to him, Gandhi likened his condition to that of the princess Draupadi in the Mahabharata when the Kauravas tried to disrobe her:

I saw your letter only now, after listening to the sweet and sad
[song] containing Draupadi's prayer... Draupadi had mighty
Bhima and Arjuna and the truthful Yudhishthira as husbands;
she was the daughter-in-law of men like Dronacharya, Bhishma
and Vidura, and yet amidst an assembly of people it appeared
she was in a terrible plight.

At that hour, she did not lose faith and prayed to God from
her heart. And God did protect her honour... Today I also am
seated in a 'palatial' house, surrounded by loving friends. Still, I
am in a sad plight. Yet there is God's help, as I find each day.

Though living in Birla House and protected by Nehru, Patel and
others in power, Gandhi too felt helpless—and aided.

Also in November, Gandhi sent a gift for the wedding of Britain's
Princess Elizabeth to Prince Philip, to whom Governor General
Louis Mountbatten was related—a small table-cloth made from thread
Gandhi had drawn on his spinning wheel. The Mountbattens took
the gift to London.

Dear Lord Mountbatten, This little thing is made out of
doubled yarn of my own spinning. The knitting was done by
a Punjabi girl who was trained by Abha's husband, my grandson.
Lady Mountbatten knows Abha. Please give the bride and the
bridegroom this with my blessings, with the wish that they
would have a long and happy life of service...

The blessing seems to have worked!

■

For the sake of body, mind and soul, Gandhi seemed to turn even
more than before to God and the utterance of God's name.

27 Sept.: My physician today, in my thought, speech and action,
is Raam, Ishwar, Rahim.

8 Nov.: [I]t is my hope that when I die I shall die with
Ramanama in my heart... I am sustained by Ramanama.

On 12 November, when Diwali, the Hindu festival of lamps and light, fell, Gandhi said:

> We must kindle the light of love within. Can you, every one of you, lay your hand on your heart and say that every sufferer, whether Hindu, Sikh or Muslim, is your own brother or sister?

On 18 November he said:

> My Raam is not a man with two hands and two feet. But if I am perfectly fit it is due to Raam's grace.

In November and December, he tried but failed to dissuade Muslims in Panipat, about 50 miles north of Delhi, from migrating to Pakistan. They did not feel safe in Panipat, their leaders finally told Gandhi. Deeply disappointed, he said to them:

> If…you want to go of your own will, no one can stop you. But you will never hear Gandhi utter the words that you should leave India. Gandhi can only tell you that you should stay, for India is your home… The Ministers have assured you that they will protect you even at the risk of their own lives. Still, if you are resolved to go and do not place any trust in their word, what can *I* do to reassure you? If I should die tomorrow, you would again have to flee…
>
> But today, having heard you and seen you, my heart weeps. Do as God guides you.

■

As 1948 opened, Gandhi was restless. His toil had not made much of a difference. When on 1 January a Thai visitor complimented him on India's independence, Gandhi remarked: 'Today not everybody can move about freely in the capital. Indian fears his brother Indian. Is this independence?'

Another disturbance was caused by a Cabinet decision to withhold the transfer of Pakistan's agreed share (Rs 55 crore, or

$115 million) of the 'sterling balance' that undivided India held at independence. Conflict in Kashmir was cited as the reason: Patel said publicly early in January that India could not hand over money to Pakistan 'for making bullets to be shot at us'. But Gandhi was not convinced that a violent dispute entitled India to keep Pakistan's money.

On 11 January he was shaken afresh when a group of Delhi's Muslims asked him to arrange their 'passage to England' as they felt unsafe in India but were opposed to Pakistan and did not wish to go there.

That Swaraj felt like a curse was the message also of a letter arriving at this time from Konda Venkatappayya of the Telugu country, a veteran freedom fighter whom Gandhi called an 'aged friend'. Writing that he was 'old, decrepit, with a broken leg, slowly limping on crutches within the walls of my house', Venkatappayya referred to the moral degradation of Congress politicians who made money by protecting criminals, and added: 'The people have begun to say that the British Government was much better'. Gandhi found the letter 'too shocking for words'.

On the morning of 12 January, however, the agitated man found peace. The 'conclusion flashed upon' him, Gandhi would say, that he must fast and not resume eating until there was 'a reunion of hearts'.

That winter afternoon, while sitting, as he put it, 'on the sun-drenched spacious Birla House lawn', Gandhi wrote out, in English, a statement announcing and explaining the fast. Sushila translated it into Hindustani and also read it out at the 5 p.m. prayer meeting, for it was Monday, Gandhi's 'silent' day.

12 Jan. 1948: Though the voice within has been beckoning for a long time, I have been shutting my ears to it lest it might be the voice of Satan...

The fast begins from the first meal tomorrow [Tuesday, 13 January]... It will end when and if I am satisfied that there is a reunion of hearts of all communities brought about without any outside pressure, but from an awakened sense of duty.

The reward will be the regaining of India's dwindling prestige... I flatter myself with the belief that the loss of her soul by India will mean the loss of the hope of the aching, storm-tossed and hungry world...

Writing to his father late at night on 12 January, Devadas, my father, pleaded against the fast:

You have surrendered to impatience...Your patient labour has saved thousands of lives... By your death you will not be able to achieve what you can by living. I would therefore beseech you to pay heed to my entreaty and give up your decision to fast.

Admitting that the son's final sentence had touched him, Gandhi asked Devadas to join in the prayer that 'the temptation to live may not lead me into a hasty or premature termination of the fast'.

A 'very much upset' Vallabhbhai Patel offered to resign if that would prevent Gandhi's fast, but Gandhi wanted Patel to continue. However, Gandhi raised with Patel the question of the Rs 55 crore. On the afternoon of 14 January the Cabinet met and decided to release the money, though Patel broke down before agreeing to the reversal.

India's solemn obligation was discharged. This decision by the Indian Cabinet, which was led by Gandhi's political 'sons', was likened by him to the change he had secured in 1932, in prison, from His Majesty's Government in London. But the Cabinet decision did not suffice. There were other conditions to be met. The fast would continue.

In his prayer talk on the evening of the 14th, Gandhi referred to Delhi's significance and to a boyhood dream:

14 Jan.: Delhi is the capital of India... It is the heart of India... All Hindus, Muslims, Sikhs, Parsis, Christians and Jews who people this country...have an equal right to it... Therefore, anyone who seeks to drive out the Muslims is Delhi's enemy

number one and therefore India's enemy number one...

When I was young I never even read the newspapers. I could read English with difficulty and my Gujarati was not satisfactory. I have had the dream ever since then that if the Hindus, Sikhs, Parsis, Christians and Muslims could live in amity not only in Rajkot but in the whole of India, they would all have a very happy life.

If that dream could be realized even now when I am an old man on the verge of death, my heart would dance. Children would then frolic in joy...

The Sikh ruler of Patiala, which had seen large-scale attacks on Muslims, asked Delhi's Sikhs to help end Gandhi's fast. A group of Hindus and Sikhs invited Muslims who had left for Karachi to return to Delhi. Prasad, the Congress president, and Azad mobilized Delhi's citizens for meeting Gandhi's terms, which had been spelt out in detail.

Activity in Delhi was matched by an unexpected response in Pakistan, where prayers were offered in public and also 'by Muslim women in the seclusion of their purda'. Leaders expressed 'deep admiration and sincere appreciation' for Gandhi's stand.

Through the Indian high commissioner in Karachi, which was then Pakistan's capital, and Pakistan's high commissioner in New Delhi, Jinnah sent a message urging Gandhi to 'live and work for the cause of Hindu-Muslim unity in the two dominions'. However, an attack on 13 January on a refugee train at West Punjab's Gujrat station killed or maimed hundreds of Hindus and Sikhs fleeing from the NWFP. Gandhi reacted realistically.

[If] this kind of thing continues in Pakistan (he said on 14 January), even if 100 men like me fasted, they would not be able to stop the tragedy that may follow.

Then, in the same remark, Gandhi challenged his people, Indians and Pakistanis, by recalling a well-known verse:

The poet says, 'If there is Paradise, it is here, it is here.' He had said it about a garden. I read it ages ago when I was a child… But Paradise is not so easily secured. If Hindus, Muslims and Sikhs become decent, become brothers, then that verse can be inscribed on every door… If that happens in Pakistan, we in India shall not be behind them…

Society is made up of individuals… If one man takes the initiative, others will follow and one can become many; if there is not even one there is nothing.

On 18 January, the sixth day of the fast, over 100 persons representing different communities and bodies called on a shrivelled Gandhi at Birla House. Rajendra Prasad read from a declaration all had signed:

We take the pledge that we shall protect the life, property and faith of the Muslims and that the incidents which have taken place in Delhi will not happen again.

We want to assure Gandhiji that the annual fair at Khwaja Qutbuddin's Mazhar will be held this year as in the previous years.

(Angry Hindus and Sikhs had earlier vowed to prevent this hoary observance, held on a revered thirteenth-century site.)

Muslims will be able to move about in Subzimandi, Karol Bagh, Paharganj and other localities just as they could in the past. The mosques which…now are in the possession of Hindus and Sikhs will be returned.

We shall not object to the return to Delhi of the Muslims who have migrated from here if they choose to come back and Muslims shall be able to carry on their business as before.

We assure that all these things will be done by our personal effort and not with the help of the police or military.

Appeals for ending the fast were then made by Prasad, Azad, Zahid Husain (the Pakistani high commissioner), Ganesh Dutt, who said he spoke for the Hindu Mahasabha and the RSS, Harbans Singh, in the name of the Sikhs, and Khurshid and M. S. Randhawa for the Delhi administration.

Acceding to the appeals, Gandhi added that he would not 'shirk another fast' if he found he had been deceived.

Brij Krishna thought that Gandhi's shrunken and lined face looked radiant.

After prayers from five faiths were sung, there was complete silence as Maulana Azad handed a glass of orange juice to Gandhi, who accepted it with a long thin hand before asking all present to partake of fruit. Among those wiping a tear was Jawaharlal, who told Gandhi he had been secretly fasting himself from the previous day.

That day, 18 January 1948, Delhi was saved for the future as a city for all. Twelve days later, Gandhi would be killed as he walked to pray on the Birla House grounds.

But the assassination only served to seal India's pledge to be a secular state, and a nation for all its citizens, a pledge largely honoured—in law if not always on the ground—in the sixty-nine years that would follow.

CHAPTER 9

THE ENDURING TRUTH IN HIS
WRITINGS

Aiming to capture Gandhi's legacy, the opening chapter suggested that one part of the legacy consists of aphorisms he left behind. A few sayings were quoted, but Gandhi the writer should be independently examined, which is the aim of this concluding chapter.

Though to his lasting regret a clash in Rajkot, just after his twenty-third birthday, with Resident Charles Ollivant scotched the literary career he had hoped for, Gandhi the author continues to stir minds worldwide through *The Story of My Experiments with Truth,* one of the best-known and most-translated autobiographies of all time.

Unusually candid though *Experiments* is, it is inevitably incomplete in the picture it offers of his life, and its story ends in any case in 1920, almost three decades before his death.

There were only two other texts he wrote as manuscripts for books. *Satyagraha in South Africa* was written during his first incarceration in India—in Pune, 1922-24. Nowhere near as widely read as the autobiography, *Satyagraha* remains an evocative and informative document on the South Africa of the late nineteenth century and early twentieth century, and on struggles waged in that period by Indians there.

A writer in English before becoming one in Gujarati, Gandhi was soon transformed into an expert author in both languages. It was in Gujarati that he wrote *Satyagraha* (which came first) as well as *Experiments* (which soon followed). To be strictly accurate, he dictated these two texts. Immediate translations into English done by close associates were revised by Gandhi before publication.

Well before these two texts, he had written *Hind Swaraj*. Much shorter than *Satyagraha* or *Experiments*, *Hind Swaraj* was composed in November 1909 on the stationery of a ship, *Kildonan Castle*, which was taking him from England to South Africa, making it possible for the American Unitarian minister, John Haynes Holmes, an ardent Gandhi admirer from 1920, to call the text a 'Sermon on the Sea'.

Books by 'M. K.' or 'Mohandas Karamchand Gandhi' bearing other titles are available in stores and online, and Mohandas Karamchand Gandhi indeed wrote the words they contain. But these books are either reproductions of talks he gave (as is the case with his scholarly yet distinctive Gita commentary), or a collection of views on a question offered by him at different times and in different places (in a newspaper or letter of his, or in a speech or conversation).

A great proportion of what he wrote and said is available in the immense archive called *Collected Works of Mahatma Gandhi,* put together over decades by a succession of dedicated scholars and now available online on the Gandhi Heritage Portal. These 100-plus volumes offer information (including on Gandhi and his associates, their projects, agreements and disputes) that historians and scholars from a variety of disciplines have mined and will continue to explore.

It is on *Hind Swaraj,* however, that this chapter will focus. Not only is *Hind Swaraj* the only theoretical text that Gandhi ever wrote; in it he explains and justifies satyagraha (without however employing that word, which in 1909 he had barely begun using), and in it he also offers his famed critique of modern or Western civilization, which he says are two different things but by which at times he appears to mean the same thing.

Let me summarize the four main suggestions I have in respect of *Hind Swaraj*.

One, I propose that *Hind Swaraj*, written in 1909 and first published in 1910, is a challenge above all to Empire, rather than to modernity. If modernity is assailed in *Hind Swaraj*, that is because modernity is a weapon of Empire, in fact Empire's most seductive weapon.

Two, in *Hind Swaraj* violence is as much Gandhi's foe as Empire.

Three, rejecting both Empire and violence, Gandhi clearly but also confidently presents in *Hind Swaraj* the theory of satyagraha, which by this time he has already tried out in practice in South Africa. If Empire and violence are the chief foes in *Hind Swaraj*, satyagraha is the manifesto's primary positive call.

Four, at the root of Gandhi's opposition to both Empire and violence is his belief in the worth of an individual human being.

When I suggest that *Hind Swaraj* is above all a challenge to Empire, I mean by Empire the domination of India and other peoples by Britain and other imperial countries like Britain, as also the domination of weak Indians by bullying Indians.

In the opening years of the twentieth century, before *Hind Swaraj* that is, Gandhi had hoped for good things from the British Empire. In his fond understanding at that time, the British Empire appeared to stand for equality among races, fair play and the rule of law.

If the British Empire was willing to give up domination and treat Indians as equals, even the *Hind Swaraj* Gandhi was ready to work with it. If the British Empire practised domination, Gandhi would fight it. It is domination and subjugation, whether practised by Europeans or Indians, that Gandhi wishes to fight, and what *Hind Swaraj* stands squarely against.

The violence that appears to be as much the foe in *Hind Swaraj* as Empire should also be understood correctly. As Anthony Parel points out, *Hind Swaraj* permits the use of force to protect the innocent from danger.

EMPIRE

All know that *Hind Swaraj* was written while Gandhi was returning from a failed mission to England. Within days of Gandhi's return to South Africa—and this is not so well known—his close colleague Henry Polak also returned, in his case from India, where, like Gandhi in England, Polak had talked about the battles of South Africa's Indian satyagrahis.

Along with a few associates, Gandhi was at Port Durban to welcome Polak. As his ship neared the pier, Polak waved from the deck. One of the welcoming party at the pier, Gandhi's colleague and relative, Chhaganlal, was waving back at Polak when a white port employee rudely asked Chhaganlal to move.

Chhaganlal moved back a step but continued to greet Polak. 'Get out!' the white employee shouted. 'Didn't you hear me? Get out!' He was about to shove Chhaganlal away when Gandhi's voice, twice as loud, was heard. 'HE SHAN'T MOVE AN INCH,' said the voice, whereupon the employee was escorted out by his colleagues.

The incident throws light on the meaning of *Hind Swaraj*. Standing on that pier, looking both at Polak on the ship's deck and at Chhaganlal on the pier, Gandhi was reacting not to the modernity of the port or of the ships parked there; he was reacting to the insulting and domineering conduct of the white employee towards an Indian. Gandhi was demanding equality for Indians, a critical component of *Hind Swaraj*.

We may doubt that in 1909 those words—'He shan't move an inch'—were often hurled at whites by an Indian in Port Durban or elsewhere in South Africa, or in fact even in India. Not in that tone anyway, and not perhaps in any tone.

Instinctively understanding that *Hind Swaraj* was taking aim at the Empire rather than at modern civilization, the British authorities in India banned the text as soon as it appeared.

Instinctively understanding that Gandhi stood for Indian equality with Europeans and for the weak Indian's equality with the dominating Indian, the Indian people took to Gandhi from the moment he appeared on the pier in Bombay in 1915, returning from South Africa.

Others were more vocal nationalists than Gandhi—not that the nationalist label is quite correct for Gandhi—but no one, not Bankim or Dayanand or Tilak or Subhas or anyone else, appears to have rejected the superiority of the West as completely and thoroughly as Gandhi did, starting with *Hind Swaraj*.

That Hinduism or Islam was superior to Christianity was indeed a claim that several Indians made, before, during and after Gandhi's lifetime, but those making that claim were willing to concede, in word or deed or both, that the India of their time was inferior and needed British or Western tutelage. While never claiming that Hinduism was superior to Christianity, Gandhi in *Hind Swaraj* washed his mind clean of the notion that India needed British or Western guidance.

Western hegemony—or Empire as I call it—was what Gandhi comprehensively rejected in *Hind Swaraj* and in his life and work, although he frequently called it Western or modern civilization, and although, doubtless, he had profound misgivings regarding that civilization.

He certainly thought that restraint was wiser than indulgence, that speed was no great judge of efficiency, that industrialization often led to new diseases and pollution, and he pointedly said so in *Hind Swaraj*. But that manifesto was not a call to return to an earlier age. It was a call to a future freed of Empire.

Gandhi is cold towards modernity because he hates subordination. Others are softened towards Empire because they are enamoured of modernity. Gandhi's starting premise is that India must have self-respect. The others' starting point is that India must become modern. With such a starting point, they become vulnerable and weak before Empire.

Not Gandhi. He will not be seduced by Empire, not by its plays, music, art, or architecture. Or by its guns and bombs. Or by contracts for guns and bombs. Once Indians find and experience Swaraj (a word with a richer meaning than anyone can easily convey), India will consider everything. Until then, he will refuse to acknowledge that the dazzling things the British have brought are good for India, be they railways, law courts or hospitals.

Let us look at what he says about the railways, which while fiercely criticized in *Hind Swaraj* were gratefully used by Gandhi for his Swaraj campaigns. 'But for the railways,' he says in *Hind Swaraj* (Chapter 9), 'the English would not have such a hold on India.' About the lawyers, who also receive short shrift in *Hind Swaraj*, he says (Chapter 11): 'The greatest injury they have done to the country is that they have tightened the English grip.' As for hospitals, Gandhi writes in *Hind Swaraj* (Chapter 12): 'The English have most certainly used the medical profession for holding us.'

It is to the Empire that he links these products of modern civilization, an Empire viewing Indians as inferior. Just before he left England for the voyage on which he wrote *Hind Swaraj*, many Britons and Indians had gathered to bid him farewell. He told them that it would be 'utterly impossible' for him to give his allegiance to 'an Empire in which he was not to be trusted...as an equal to any other member of the Empire'.

Gandhi's simple and matter-of-fact assumption of equality with the West comes across from any number of encounters. Take this one, in Delhi, between him and Western and Indian reporters at the end of the successful Gandhi-Irwin talks in March 1931:

Journalist: Will you press for Purna Swaraj, complete independence, at the Round Table Conference?
Gandhi: We will deny our very existence if we do not press for it.... The word Swaraj is a sacred word, a Vedic word, meaning self-rule and self-restraint, and not freedom from all restraint which 'independence' often means.

Journalist: What was it that turned the tide in the negotiations?
Gandhi (smiling): Goodness on the part of Lord Irwin and perhaps (*a bigger smile on Gandhi*) equal goodness on my part as well.

Journalist: What is your idea of 'Purna Swaraj?' Would it be possible within the British Empire?

Gandhi: It would be possible but on terms of absolute equality. Complete independence may mean separation and popular imagination does understand it in that light. But, if we remain part of the Commonwealth, on terms of absolute equality, instead of Downing Street being the centre of the Empire, Delhi should be the centre.

India has a population of 300 million and that is a factor that cannot be ignored. Friends suggest that England will never be able to reconcile itself to that position. But I do not despair. The British are a practical people and as they love liberty for themselves, it is only a step further to desire the same liberty for others.

That Gandhi was ready to talk, deal and trade with the West but only as an equal is what India understood and loved, and that is what made its mark on the world as well. That is what *Hind Swaraj* spelt out, and that perhaps is the secret of Gandhi's continuing impact on Native Americans, Blacks in the US, Africans, Latin Americans, Okinawans, Arabs, and others who felt the heel of European domination.

The passion for equality was joined to agitation in his heart at 'India's sad condition' under imperialism. 'In thinking of it,' he says in *Hind Swaraj*, 'my eyes water and my throat gets parched.' He doubts that he can ever fully 'explain what is in my heart'.

In 1931, when shortly after his talks with Irwin he travelled via the Suez Canal for talks in London, Egyptians resentful of European hegemony turned up at Suez and Port Said. They were not allowed to meet the Empire's chief rebel. The poet Ahmad Shawqi had exhorted Egyptians that as Gandhi passed by they should...

Stop to welcome him, from close quarters sitting in boats and also from a distance in whatever way possible. He is a guide and pathfinder like Confucius... He has inspired in Hindus and Muslims the spirit of mutual love and with his spiritual powers brought the two swords in one sheath. He is a great powerhouse which generates the power to tame predators.

Welcome and honour Gandhi, Shawqi says, because he has tamed predators, even the predator that was dictating to Egypt.

Another delightful example of Gandhi's passion against Empire is the previously mentioned letter he wrote on 27/28 June 1947 to Mountbatten right after an interview in which Mountbatten had apparently said that if Congress leaders were not helpful enough over the details of Partition, Independence might not after all occur on 15 August.

In his letter Gandhi first referred to divide-and-rule and to 'the initial mistake of the British being party to splitting India into two'—a mistake to which now, this is end-June 1947, a disappointed Gandhi had resigned himself. Then Gandhi said that he had been 'startled' by the apparent threat: as if dividing India was not enough, you now want to go back on your word on the date of independence?

In reply, Mountbatten claimed he had been misinterpreted. No, he said, we are not talking of staying on after 15 August. Gandhi had asserted his equality, his independence—his *Hind Swaraj*, one can say—directly challenging a viceroy who also was a once and future admiral with command over warships.

But forty years earlier, too, Gandhi had done just that, in *Hind Swaraj*. Its last chapter, titled 'Emancipation' in the Gujarati version but simply 'Conclusion' in the English version, has the following lines. Asked 'what, then, would you say to the English,' Gandhi (styling himself as 'Editor') replies:

> To them I would respectfully say... [A]lthough you are the rulers, you will have to remain as servants of the people. It is not we who have to do as you wish, but it is you who have to do as we wish. You may keep the riches that you have drained away from this land, but you may not drain riches henceforth...
>
> If [our] submissions be not acceptable to you, we cease to

play the ruled. You may, if you like, cut us to pieces. You may
shatter us at the cannon's mouth. If you act contrary to our
will, we will not help you, and without our help we know
that you cannot move one step forward.

At no time was Gandhi's opposition to Empire, and his commitment
to equality for the people of India, clearer, or more impassioned,
than in 1942. Even though it was Hitler and Nazism that the Allies
were fighting, he would not abandon the people of India or their
self-respect by suspending India's struggle for Swaraj against a key
member of the Allies. That struggle was necessary. After all Churchill
had made it plain in September 1941 that the Atlantic Charter
assuring post-war independence would not apply to India.

Recalling that Britons had evacuated Malaya and Burma and
that the Empire would, if it came to that, evacuate every British
man, woman and child from India, Gandhi added in Mumbai on
8 August 1942:

Where shall I go and where shall I take the forty crores of
India? How is this vast mass of humanity to be aflame in the
cause of world-deliverance?.. If lustre is to be put into their
eyes, freedom has to come not tomorrow but today. I have,
therefore, pledged the Congress and the Congress has pledged
herself that she will do or die.

Gandhi wrote *Hind Swaraj* in 1909 and launched Quit India in 1942
for the sake of his people in *his* time, for their bodies and their spirit,
and, in his words, for their future role in world—deliverance—not
for the sake of a supposed way of life that in parts of *Hind Swaraj*
he says flourished in India's ancient past.

■

The Gandhi who wrote *Hind Swaraj* had an intimate knowledge of
violence. He had taken at least three violent attacks on his person
(from whites in Durban in January 1897; from fellow Indians in

Johannesburg in February 1908; and, later in 1908, from an African fellow-prisoner in Johannesburg's Fort prison). In 1899 during the Boer War and again in 1906 during the Zulu rebellion he had led an Indian ambulance unit into the battlefield.

Looking at and nursing gashes on the bodies of humans, often humans who had nothing to do with the clash in which they were caught, Gandhi had absorbed the reality of war and violence. He understood these realities better than Europe-based radical Indian expatriates who in 1906 and again in 1909 had spoken to Gandhi of their fascination with violence and assassinations.

Moreover, the Gandhi who wrote *Hind Swaraj* was also a man who three years earlier, during that experience in the Zulu country, had realized clearly that his task was to demonstrate the power of satyagraha to the world. In order to free and equip himself for such a task, he had embraced, at that time in Zululand, the vows of chastity and poverty.

It was this Gandhi, one with an intimate awareness of what violence does and a readiness to demonstrate satyagraha, who spoke about the violence of war in London in October 1909, a few weeks before he wrote *Hind Swaraj*.

In London in 1906 and again in 1909, and in South Africa between 1906 and 1909, Gandhi had encountered Indian votaries or defenders of assassination, including (in London) Shyamji Krishnavarma and Vinayak Savarkar, and (in Johannesburg) Mir Alam and his associates. He had also closely followed incidents in India of violent attempts on the lives of some Britons.

There is enough evidence that among other things *Hind Swaraj* was Gandhi's response to the fascination of many young Indians, including highly educated and westernized ones, with extremist violence. Shortly before Gandhi's 1909 arrival in England, an Indian student in London, Madanlal Dhingra, had killed Sir William Curzon-Wyllie, political aide to Lord Morley, the Secretary of State for India.

Writing from London in his journal in South Africa, *Indian Opinion*, Gandhi condemned the assassination and refuted the thinking behind it. A year earlier, after a bomb had taken white lives in India, Gandhi had said that if killers in India succeeded in driving out the British, they, the killers, would become autocratic rulers. Gandhi wrote:

> If all the British were to be killed, those who kill them would become the masters of India, and as a result India would continue in a state of slavery.

In his comment on Dhingra's deed, he repeated the argument:

> Even should the British leave in consequence of such murderous acts, who will rule in their place? Is the Englishman bad because he is an Englishman? Is it that everyone with an Indian skin is good? If that is so, there should be [no] angry protest against oppression by Indian princes. India can gain nothing from the rule of murderers—no matter whether they are black or white. Under such a rule, India will be utterly ruined and laid waste.

The argument was spelt out in *Hind Swaraj*, where the 'Editor' (Gandhi) tells the 'Reader', who mouths the reasoning of the extremists, that what was needed was Swaraj or self-rule for India's millions, not a change of masters. Adds Gandhi:

> How can the millions obtain self-rule? You will admit that people under several Indian princes are being ground down. The latter mercilessly crush them. Their tyranny is greater than that of the English…Do you not tremble to think of freeing India by assassination?… Whom do you suppose to free by assassination? (*You don't want anyone else's freedom, Gandhi is saying to the militants, you only want power for yourselves.*) The millions of India do not desire it… Those who will rise to power by murder will certainly not make the nation happy.

Years later, in 1931, after young people across India had been stirred by Bhagat Singh's hanging for the killing of Saunders, a police officer, Gandhi said, 'One's head bends before Bhagat Singh's bravery and sacrifice.' Yet he told the Indian people:

But I want you also to realize Bhagat Singh's error... I declare that we cannot win Swaraj for our famishing millions, for our deaf and dumb, for our lame and crippled, by the way of the sword. With the Most High as witness I want to proclaim this truth...

Gandhi was warning that in a land that privileged killing, the weak would be bullied by the well-armed, the well-heeled and the strong-bodied. Author Gandhi wants no domination of Indians by other Indians, no Indian imperialism over Indians or non-Indians. He knows that the heel of Empire can belong also to an Indian foot.

As he said in *Hind Swaraj*, 'My patriotism does not teach me that I am to allow people to be crushed under the heel of Indian princes'. Here 'prince' clearly stands for any dominating or cruel Indian.

■

If love of violence was a threat to the poor and the crippled, nonviolence could become a threat to Empire, says *Hind Swaraj*. How? By aligning itself with struggle. Nonviolence plus struggle is satyagraha. When individuals who are 'intensely dissatisfied with the present pitiable condition' so shape themselves that 'they will not cower before brute force and will not, on any account, desire to use brute force', they become satyagrahis.

Gandhi freely conceded that satyagraha requires courage. A satyagrahi 'will say he will not obey a law against his conscience even though he may be blown to pieces at the mouth of a cannon'. It was more courageous 'with a smiling face to approach a cannon and be blown to pieces' than to blow 'others to pieces from behind a cannon'.

A seemingly tough person may lack courage, while a crippled one may show it. That is only one of the several beauties of satyagraha. As *Hind Swaraj* puts it:

Even a man weak in body is capable of offering this resistance. One man can offer it just as well as millions. (*Gandhi's declaration in* Hind Swaraj *that he for one was resolved to offer it was part of* Hind Swaraj*'s appeal.*) Both men and women can indulge in [satyagraha]... [It] is an all-sided sword; it can be used anyhow; it blesses him who uses it and him against whom it is used. Without drawing a drop of blood, it produces far-reaching results. It never rusts, and cannot be stolen... It does not require a scabbard.

We know that the strong as well as the seemingly weak joined the satyagrahas that later took place in South Africa and in India. In 1931, speaking of the Salt March, Gandhi could say:

Do you think that all the women and the children who covered themselves with glory during the last campaign would have done so if we had pursued the path of violence?

Would our women, known as the meekest on earth, would women like Gangabehn, who withstood the lathi-blows until her white sari was drenched in blood, have done the unique service they did if we had violence in us?

And our children—our vanarasena. How could you have had these innocent ones, who renounced their toys, their kites and their crackers, and joined as soldiers of Swaraj—how could you have enlisted them in a violent struggle? We were able to enlist as soldiers millions of men, women and children because we were pledged to non-violence.

Another argument for nonviolence was mentioned in *Hind Swaraj*. Since we may be mistaken in our views, let us never kill for them, even though we must fight for them: 'No man can claim to be absolutely in the right, or that a particular thing is wrong, because he thinks so.'

In addition, Gandhi claimed in *Hind Swaraj* that 'brute force is not natural to the Indian soil'. He was trying to suggest that violence was natural to an industrialized, modernized West, not to India. Aware that a few young Indians had come to Europe at about this time to learn bomb-making and find arms for militants in India, he was keen to change their thinking, if that were possible, and to point out flaws in their views.

These young pro-violence Indians were greatly taken with aspects of the West. They wanted a westernized, strong in arms but Indian-ruled India, while Gandhi wanted, he said, an India true to her own roots, content with her way of life, and committed to peace. Gandhi enjoyed, agreed with, and reproduced lines about Indian nationalists that G. K. Chesterton had published while Gandhi was in England in 1909:

> When I see...the views of Indian nationalists, I get bored and feel dubious about them. What they want is not very Indian and not very national... Suppose an Indian said: 'I wish India had always been free from white men and all their works. Everything has its own faults and we prefer our own... I prefer dying in battle to dying in [a Western] hospital... If you (the British) do not like our way of living, we never asked you to. Go, and leave us with it.'
>
> Supposing an Indian said that, I should call him an Indian nationalist. He would be an authentic Indian... But the Indian nationalists whose works I have read go on saying: 'Give me a ballot box. Give me the judge's wig. I have a natural right to be Prime Minister. My soul is starved if I am excluded from the editorship of the *Daily Mail*.' Even the most sympathetic person may say in reply: 'What you say is very fine, my good Indian, but it is we who invented these things.'

So Gandhi claimed to see Indianness in his nonviolence and Westernness in the pro-violence views of his young rivals. But, as we know, Gandhi's assumption that violence was something foreign to India was deeply shaken before the end of his life. In November 1946 he would confess to a visitor in violence-hit Noakhali:

> When I was in detention in the Aga Khan Palace, I once sat down to write a thesis on India as a protagonist of non-

violence. But as I proceeded with my writing, I could not go
on. I had to stop.

He stopped because the reality of violence in the history of India did
not permit him to treat Indian belief in nonviolence as the dominant
reality. And we know too that in 1936 he told African-American
visitors that he thought it would be American Blacks who would
'deliver the message of unadulterated nonviolence to the world'.

Gandhi's nonviolence valued fraternity as much as it valued
equality. With all his passion for Indian equality with the West, and
for the equal dignity that, he felt, all religions and cultures demanded,
Hindu or Islamic or Indian supremacy was *never* Gandhi's position. He
stood for friendship and goodwill among the cultures and civilizations
of the world.

Also, his nonviolence was nonviolence in word, thought and deed.
It sought to bar not only killing but also hating or harming. Decades
later in America, in November 1957, when Martin Luther King, Jr.,
and his African-American colleagues accepted the motto, 'Not one
hair of one head of one white person shall be harmed,' they recalled
Gandhi and his 1936 remark about what Black Americans could do.

Thus in Gandhi's unadulterated nonviolence, as King and his
associates clearly saw, 'don't harm one hair' was joined to 'don't yield
one inch'. Love and toughness were two sides of the satyagraha coin.

■

We know that *Hind Swaraj* featured in the interesting Gandhi–Nehru
discussion of October–November 1945. Initiated by Gandhi, the
exchange occurred in talks and letters. Since we have no record of
the talks, which however are taken for granted in the letters, the
latter by themselves do not take us very far. It is clear, however, that
Gandhi said during this interaction that he stood by *Hind Swaraj*,
with Nehru maintaining that he stood by his disagreement with
it. In this exchange both said they lacked a copy of *Hind Swaraj*
to refer to!

But the two seemed to agree on the importance of the individual. Gandhi wrote:

> In [the] village of my dreams the villager will not be dull—he will be all awareness. He will not live like an animal in filth and darkness. Men and women will live in freedom, prepared to face the whole world. There will be no plague, no cholera and no smallpox. Nobody will be allowed to be idle or to wallow in luxury...
>
> The sum and substance of what I want to say is that the individual person should have control over the things that are necessary for the sustenance of life. If he cannot have such control the individual cannot survive. Ultimately, the world is made up only of individuals.

An individual living in freedom and health and ready to face the whole world—this is the heart of Gandhi's vision. We saw that in *Hind Swaraj* he spoke of the primacy of the satyagrahi's conscience. The satyagrahi would bend the knee before that conscience but not before cannons or empires. This was Gandhi's truth right from *Hind Swaraj* until his last days. About two weeks before he was killed, a Gandhi embarked on his final fast said:

> Society is made up of individuals. It is we that make society...
> If one man takes the initiative others will follow and one can become many; if there is not even one there is nothing.

From the right of an individual to heed his or her conscience descended the rights of minorities. Says *Hind Swaraj*: 'Many examples can be given in which acts of majorities will be found to have been wrong, and those of minorities to have been right. All reforms owe their origin to the [initiatives] of minorities in opposition to majorities'.

The freedom of the press too was only an aspect of the freedom of the individual. When in 1940 Gandhi was ordered not to report in his journals the arrest of Vinoba Bhave at the start of an individual civil disobedience campaign, Gandhi suspended the journals' publication and wrote:

> Let everyone become his own walking newspaper and carry the good news from mouth to mouth... The idea here is of my telling my neighbour what I have authentically heard. This no Government can overtake or suppress. It is the cheapest newspaper yet devised and it defies the wit of Government, however clever it may be.
>
> Let these walking newspapers be sure of the news they give. They should not indulge in any idle gossip. They should make sure of the source of information, and they will find that the public gets all the information that they need without opening their morning newspaper...

These lines seem to anticipate, and propose norms for, the social media of the 2010s.

In 1942, at the launch of Quit India, Gandhi claimed that Indians who obeyed the principles of satyagraha and were united for the nation's independence would pioneer something finer than what had been produced elsewhere:

> If you want real freedom you will have to come together and...create true democracy— democracy the like of which has not been so far witnessed...
>
> I have read a good deal about the French revolution. Carlyle's works I read while in jail. I have great admiration for the French people. Pandit Jawaharlal has told me all about the Russian revolution. But I hold that though theirs was a fight for the people it was not a fight for real democracy which I envisaged.
>
> My democracy means every man is his own master. I have read sufficient history and I did not see such an experiment on so large a scale for the establishment of democracy by non-violence.

Every person possessing and experiencing Swaraj or self-rule: from *Hind Swaraj* onwards, that was the heart of Gandhi's vision. In July 1946, in a comment in *Harijan,* he spelt out his ideal structure for an Indian Union:

> In this structure composed of innumerable villages, there will be ever-widening, never-ascending circles. Life will not be a pyramid with the apex sustained by the bottom. But it will be an oceanic circle whose centre will be the individual always ready to perish for the village, the latter ready to perish for the circle of villages, till at last the whole becomes one life composed of individuals, never aggressive in their arrogance but ever humble, sharing the majesty of the oceanic circle of which they are integral units.
>
> Therefore the outermost circumference will not wield power to crush the inner circle but will give strength to all within and derive its own strength from it.

An individual's task is to be conscious of other individuals, each of whom constitutes 'the centre of an oceanic circle'. And a quest for empowering others in need is the solution to every doubt and anxiety, as Gandhi famously wrote (as we saw earlier) in Kolkata in August 1947, the month of India's political Swaraj:

> I will give you a talisman. Whenever you are in doubt, or when the self becomes too much with you, apply the following test. Recall the face of the poorest and the weakest man whom you may have seen, and ask yourself if the step you contemplate is going to be of any use to him. Will he gain anything by it? Will it restore him to a control over his own life and destiny? In other words, will it lead to Swaraj for the hungry and spiritually starving millions? Then you will find your doubts and yourself melting away.

■

That much that passed for industrial and technological advance was deceptive was an early and lasting belief with Gandhi. It predated *Hind Swaraj*. Examples are easy to give. Within a year of his arrival in South Africa he had written pejoratively (in the *Natal Mercury)* of 'the dazzling and bright surface of modern civilization'.

The following year he referred (in the *Natal Advertiser*) to 'the utter inadequacy of materialism' and of 'a civilization [whose] greatest achievements are the invention of the most terrible weapons of destruction'. On 20 August 1903 he had written in *Indian Opinion* of 'the tinsel splendour of modern civilization'.

But that his misgivings on the supposed virtues of technological advance could be integrated into his political philosophy was a new insight for Gandhi, an insight that contributed to Gandhi's feeling, while writing *Hind Swaraj,* that he was on to something major.

What contributed even more to that feeling was Gandhi's additional insight, a brilliant one, that with a critique of modernity he could capture the platform of Indian nationalism. The formula that violence and Western civilization went together and were ranged against satyagraha and Indian civilization was most promising.

It could unite Indians and put the Empire on the defensive. Equally importantly, it could weaken and marginalize the school of violence and terrorism that was gaining adherents in India, among Indian expatriates in the West, and among Indians in South Africa.

As we have seen, it was always Gandhi's deep belief that harms flow from a love of speed, size and instant gratification. This preference for the Simple Life (to use this shorthand for Gandhi's view on industrialization) had contributed to the poverty vow he had taken in 1906 in the Zulu country. But how fortunate for Gandhi that his personal preference provided the basis for a magnificent political strategy.

No wonder Gandhi exuded confidence, and referred excitedly to his 'discovery' when writing to Polak and Hermann Kallenbach, his closest colleagues at the time. Anyone would jump with joy when her or his ardent personal bias translates into a deadly political arrow.

After having integrated his preference for the Simple Life into

Hind Swaraj's clear-cut worldview, there was no way in which Gandhi could amend that worldview, or admit that it was oversimplified, without confusing everyone and damaging his purpose.

Gandhi the communicator needed to reach and enlist millions who had neither the time nor the ability to read long nuanced texts replete with 'on the one hand' this and 'on the other hand' that, 'broadly speaking' and 'by and large', phrases that appealed to Nehru, who frequently used them. Gandhi, on the other hand, had to present stark binaries to the millions he sought to reach and enlist: truth vs. untruth, ahimsa vs. war, rough khadi vs. smooth cloth, nature cure vs. hospitalization, the march-on-foot vs. tanks, satyagraha vs. assassination, India vs. the Empire, the charkha vs. the battleship, the man with a walking stick vs. the atom bomb.

Nuanced, revised and corrected editions of *Hind Swaraj* would have pleased Gandhi's critics— and destroyed Gandhi's credibility, which rested on the simplicity and clarity of his message. This damage to the clarity of his message he would not allow. Nor was he willing to give up, through dilution or qualifications, the political potency of the position that satyagraha and the Indian way went together, as did violence and the Western way.

As if repeating his 1909 Port Durban declaration, he said in effect, 'I shan't give an inch to the critics of *Hind Swaraj*.'

The most he would say, whenever a Nehru or a G. Ramachandran or a G. D. Birla confronted him over *Hind Swaraj,* was that he might change a word here or a comma there but he stood by its central message.

That central message, the truth of *Hind Swaraj,* was not opposition to tall buildings or large factories or the generation of electricity or to any better image of modernity. It was opposition to Empire and violence, to domination of the weak by the strong. Gandhi was probably justified in standing by that central message.

We in our time, however, can concede that it is hard to justify a secondary message of *Hind Swaraj,* namely that satyagraha and the Indian way go together, as do violence and the Western way.

Domination and violence are neither Western nor Eastern. Yet they should be resisted. And satyagraha, when conceived in wisdom and offered with discipline, may be the finest resistance in both East and West. This truth of *Hind Swaraj* is greater—it is truer—than the theory about the distribution of violence between East and West.

Hind Swaraj also, of course, contains pertinent and prescient warnings against hurting our planet through reckless industrialization or 'development'. Though couched in sweeping language, Gandhi's case in *Hind Swaraj* for the Simple Life holds critical importance today. We know that what he opposed was not technology but its misuse through greed. A hundred years ago he warned fellow human beings against an unchecked desire for more—an unchecked desire for more mass manufacturing, among other things. A hundred years ago, when industrialization dazzled most people, Gandhi spoke out for fresh air, clean water and the power of the village. Still, we should not forget the political use that Gandhi made of his love for the Simple Life.

A radical text like *Hind Swaraj* does things and means things its author may not have intended. Decades after it was first written, others can and do mix their own meanings into *Hind Swaraj*. This is a compliment to the text and need not be lamented. As far as Gandhi was concerned, however, I have argued that his intention with *Hind Swaraj* was less to initiate a debate over modernity or technology and more to initiate a debate over Empire, violence and satyagraha.

Let me add that while questions of technology and the environment are more important today than ever before, Empire, domination and violence have not lost their importance. Today's Empires, whether or not headed constitutionally by monarchs, also seek to dominate, and yes, they exist in more than one region of our world. And today's extremists, like their predecessors, also seek to pursue their goals through assassination.

So there is need to continue to listen to *Hind Swaraj*.

And there may be value in reading Gandhi in texts other than *Hind Swaraj,* including the text offered by his life, which these pages have tried to summarize.

NOTES AND REFERENCES

INTRODUCTION: WHY GANDHI STILL MATTERS

ix **If Gandhi was all that persons like Einstein and Tagore**: Einstein's, Tagore's and King's comments are mentioned in the ensuing text. Gokhale spoke as follows at the Lahore session of the Indian National Congress in 1909: 'It is one of the privileges of my life that I know Mr. Gandhi personally, and I can tell you that a purer, nobler, a braver and a more exalted spirit has never moved on this earth… [He] is a man among men, a hero among heroes, a patriot among patriots, and we may well say that in him Indian humanity at the present time has really reached its high watermark.' G. K. Gokhale, *Speeches and Writings of G. K. Gokhale,* D. G. Karve and D. V. Ambedkar (eds.), Bombay: Asia Publishing House, 1966, volume 2, p. 420.

x **'the preponderating impression he leaves is not sweetness but strength'**: E. Stanley Jones, *Gandhi,* Nashville: Abingdon, 1948, pp. 33–34.

CHAPTER 1: THE LEGACY OF GANDHI

2 **'stopped at the threshold of huts of thousands of the dispossessed'**: *Modern Review,* Calcutta, October 1920; Sisir Kumar Das (ed.), *Selected English Writings of Rabindranath Tagore,* volume 2, New Delhi: Sahitya Akademi, 1994, p. 547.

2 **Raised in a privileged family in Rajkot in western India**: Joseph J. Doke, *M. K. Gandhi: An Indian Patriot in South Africa,* New Delhi: Publications Division, 1967, p. 19.

5 **'an immensely tall figure with an absolutely straight back'**: Rajmohan Gandhi, *Ghaffar Khan: Nonviolent Badshah of the Pashtuns,* New Delhi: Penguin Viking, 2004, p. 1.

6 **[Bacon] told me, 'Ghani, I was the Assistant Commissioner'** Omar Khan, Interview with Ghani Khan, 19 May 1990, www.harappa.com.

6 **The sight of an Englishman [used to] frighten us**: Dinanath Gopal Tendulkar, *Abdul Ghaffar Khan: Faith is a Battle,* Bombay: Popular Prakashan, 1967, pp. 253–254.

7 **The British crushed the violent movement in no time**: Ibid, p. 161.

7 **'almost unintelligible on the Frontier where most men carry firearms'**:

Sir Reginald Coupland, *The Indian Problem, Part II*, London: Oxford University Press, 1944, p. 22.

7   **But when Ghaffar Khan asked Pashtuns to shed all weapons and join a non-violent struggle:** Tendulkar, *Abdul Ghaffar Khan*, pp. 327-328.

7   **'coming from strong and fearless men,' was 'very unexpected':** Halide Edib, *Inside India*, London: Allen & Unwin, 1937, p. 336; cited in Joan Bondurant, *Conquest of Violence*, Princeton: Princeton University Press, 1988, p. 140.

7   **'whose self-detonations invite devastating retaliatory assaults on their innocent fellow citizens':** Harold Gould, *Indian Express*, 20 June 2003.

8   **If they are idol worshippers, what are we?:** Mahadev Desai, *Two Servants of God*, New Delhi: Hindustan Times Press, 1935, pp. 40-41.

8   **Some people mislead you in the name of Islam:** Tendulkar, *Abdul Ghaffar Khan*, pp. 419-21.

9   **[Gandhi] was able to achieve for his people independence from the domination of the British Empire:** Palm Sunday Sermon on Mohandas K. Gandhi, Delivered at Dexter Avenue Baptist Church, Montgomery, Ala, 22 March 1959. See: http://kingencyclopedia.stanford.edu/encyclopedia/documentsentry/palm_sunday_sermon_on_mohandas_k_gandhi.1.html

10   **'[Dr. Johnson's] message was so profound and electrifying':** Sudarshan Kapur, *Raising Up a Prophet: The African-American Encounter with Gandhi*, New Delhi: Oxford University Press, 1993, p. 147.

10   **'lift[ing] the love ethic of Jesus above mere interaction between individuals':** Stephen B. Oates, *Let the Trumpet Sound: The Life of Martin Luther King, Jr*, New York: Harper & Row, 1982, p. 31.

10   **Well, if it comes true:** *Collected Works of Mahatma Gandhi, 62:202.*

14   **I accept [the prize] as a tribute to the man who founded the modern tradition of non-violent:** The 14th Dalai Lama's Acceptance Speech, on the occasion of the award of the Nobel Peace Prize in Oslo, 10 December 1989. See: https://www.nobelprize.org/nobel_prizes/peace/laureates/1989/lama-acceptance_en.html.

14   **Even if the democracy movement were to succeed through force of arms:** Aung San Suu Kyi, *The Voice of Hope: Conversations with Alan Clements*, New York: Seven Stories Press, 1997, pp. 25-26.

17   **'breeding grounds for warlords' and for 'militarism, coups, uprisings, and civil wars':** B. R. Nanda, *Mahatma Gandhi: A Biography*, New Delhi: Oxford University Press, 1996, p. 406.

CHAPTER 2: GANDHI'S PASSIONS

21   **A leader of his people, unsupported by any outside authority:** Albert Einstein, *Out of My Later Years: The Scientist, Philosopher, and Man Portrayed Through his Own Words*, New York: Philosophical Library, 1950, p. 240.

22   **The deliverance of India from British rule, which admittedly was Gandhi's chief political aim:** Penderel Moon, *Gandhi and Modern India*, New York: W. W. Norton & Company, 1969, p. 289.

23   'White Christianity stood before Gandhi the other day': Kapur, *Raising Up a Prophet*, p. 40.

23   Let not the 12 million [African- Americans] be ashamed: Ibid, p. 39.

24   What we need in America is a Gandhi: Ibid, p. 66.

24   'soothed them and lifted them above their sorrows': Nirmal Kumar Bose, *Lectures on Gandhism*, Ahmedabad: Navajivan Publishing, 1971, p. 63.

25   Invite a Harijan every day to dine with you: Dinanath Gopal Tendulkar, *Mahatma; life of Mohandas Karamchand Gandhi*, 7: 350; also *CW*, 93: 229.

26   In the three-quarters of the country: *CW*, 95: 286-7.

27   If a bath could not be easily had, Mohan was to cancel the 'unholy touch': *CW*, 23:42.

27   Here, let us merely note that after Pakistanis heard on the evening of 30 January 1948: 'Kitchen fires were not lit that night in many homes in Pakistan.' Raza Kasim, in Lahore, to the author, 1994.

27   Each one of us who has raised his hand against innocent men: *Homage to Mahatma*, New Delhi: Publications Division, 1949, p. 27.

27   They killed him, this man who had galvanized 400 million [Indians]: On 22 March 1959. *The Papers of Martin Luther King, Jr.*, Berkeley: University of California Press, 1992, volume 5, p. 156.

28   'God Himself breathed it into your mind': Manu Gandhi, *Ekla Chalo Re*, Ahmedabad: Navajivan Publishing, 1957, pp. 91-92.

29   'never even read the newspapers, could read English with difficulty': *CW*, 98: 235.

29   'their pride went before destruction': *CW*, 40: 70.

30   young Gandhi participated in meetings in London of the Anjuman-e-Islam: James D. Hunt, *Gandhi in London*, New Delhi: Promilla, 1978, p. 13.

30   We know the name of at least one Muslim student he befriended: D. G. Tendulkar, *Gandhi in Champaran*, New Delhi: Publications Division, 1994 (first edition 1957), p. 27.

30   And we know that in London Gandhi noticed that some Muslim students: 'I had evidence of [Pan-Islamism] even while I was a student in England many years ago.' Remark to Muslim leaders in Bengal in May 1947, *CW*, 87:442-443.

31   'cannot be above reason and morality': *CW*, 14: 345.

31   It is no good quoting verses: *CW*, 14: 73-77.

33   The spindle in Gandhi's hand became sharper than the sword: Edited from quotation by Omar el-Haqqaq in *Mahatma Gandhi: 125 Years*, B. R. Nanda (ed.), New Delhi: Indian Council for Cultural Relations, 1995, p. 80.

35   I have to cruelly suppress my urges: Mahadev Desai, *Day-to-day with Gandhi*, Varanasi: Sarva Seva Sangh, volume 1, pp. 1:56-57, 182.

35   'You will see, my dear Mr Shirer!': William L. Shirer, *Gandhi: A Memoir*, New Delhi: Rupa Publications, 1993, p. 60.

35   'Gandhi's was the most colossal experiment in world history': Quoted

in C. F. Andrews, 'Heart Beats in India', *Asia*, March 1930, p. 198.

35 **'Such humiliation and defiance':** Churchill's remark in the House of Commons on 12 March 1931 can be seen in *Winston Churchill: His Complete Speeches*, Robert Rhodes James (ed.), New York: Chelsea House, volume V (1928-1935), 1974, p. 4995.

36 **'By far the most serious rebellion since that of 1857':** Linlithgow to Churchill, 31 August 1942. Linlithgow Papers, F 125/58, London: India Office Library.

36 **Even if I stand alone, I swear by non-violence and truth:** *CW,* 88: 226.

37 **All the Asian representatives have come together:** *CW,* 94: 212.

38 **In this age of democracy, in this age of awakening of the poorest of the poor:** *CW,* 94: 222-23.

38 **I must not yield to the temptation:** *CW,* 96: 209.

38 **The young men were 'completely won over' by this offer:** Pyarelal, *Mahatma Gandhi: The Last Phase*, volume 2, pp. 367-368.

39 **In their thousands [Calcutta's residents] began to embrace one another:** From article of 16 August by Gandhi in *Harijan*, 24 August 1947; 96: 236-37.

39 **My dear Agatha:** *CW,* 96: 230-31

39 **the joy of fraternization:** From article of 16 August by Gandhi in *Harijan*, 24 August 1947; 96: 236-37

39 **'treat the Europeans who stayed in India with the same regard':** *CW,* 96: 232.

40 **'On the streets he heard, from the joint throats of Hindus and Muslims:** *CW,* 96: 236-37.

CHAPTER 3: GANDHI'S GIFT AND HIS GOD

43 **'The Indians and other blacks':** The Gujarati word 'kalo' translated as 'coloured' in the *Collected Works* (English), has been retranslated here as 'black'.

43 **'have much to ponder and act with circumspection':** *Indian Opinion*, 7 April 1906; *CW,* 5: 162.

44 **'To the governor of Natal, Gandhi offered, with (as he put it) 'the community's permission':** M. K. Gandhi, *Satyagraha in South Africa*, Ahmedabad: Navajivan Publishing, 1929, p. 90.

44 **'at a time like this we should all refrain from discussing them':** Dube's remark quoted from Andre Odendaal, *Vukani Bantu*, 1984, p. 70; in E.S. Reddy, *Gandhiji: Vision of a Free South Africa*, New Delhi: Sanchar, 1995, p. 21.

45 **'both a deeper identification with the maltreated and a stronger':** Erik H. Erikson, *Gandhi's Truth: On the Origins of Militant Nonviolence*, New York: W. W. Norton & Company, 1993.

46 **'A mission...came to me in 1906':** Letter of 31 December 1942 to Linlithgow; *CW,* 83: 274-6.

46 **'My people were excited':** Speech in Birmingham, England, 18 October 1931; *Young India*, 5 November 1931, *CW,* 54: 47.

46 **'I can boldly declare, and with certainty, that so long as':** *CW,* 5: 335.

47 'Gandhi proceeded in exactly the opposite direction': Jonathan Schell, *The Unconquerable World: Power, Nonviolence, and the Will of the People*, New York: Metropolitan, 2003, pp. 114–115.

48 'You want them to be saints before they are men': Erikson, *Gandhi's Truth*, p. 316.

49 'Sometimes love's anguish left deep scars on the loved ones': *Young India*, 9 April 1924.

49 'You will both earn your bread by the sweat of your brow': Dinanath Gopal Tendulkar, *Mahatma*, 2: 405.

50 I have some interests which I cannot satisfy: *CW,* 63: 417-421, 31 October and 2 November, 1936.

51 Most callers in the final fifteen years of his life thought that Gandhi looked youthful: Martin Green, *Gandhi: Voice of a New Age Revolution*, New York: Continuum, 1993, p. 346.

51 He smiled, grinned, chuckled, crackled, or laughed heartily: Ibid.

51 In no time at all Gandhi had us all laughing and completely at our ease: Homer Jack, *The Gandhi Reader*, New York: Grove Press, 1956, p. 399.

51 'Sardar Vallabhbhai is with me. His jokes make me laugh': Narhari Parikh, *Sardar Vallabhbhai Patel*, volume 2, Ahmedabad: Navajivan Publishing, 1971, pp. 91–92.

52 'I always felt deeply moved in his presence': Green, *Gandhi*.

52 'Saraladevi's company is very endearing': *CW,* 19: 84, 27 October 1919.

53 Rajagopalachari warned Gandhi that he was nursing 'a most dreadful delusion': Letter of 16 June 1920 from Madras, with Gopal Gandhi, Kolkata.

53 Thirteen years later, in 1933, Gandhi would say that he had been saved: To Father William Lash and E. Stanley Jones; *CW,* 59: 196 and 227.

53 'put in one pan all the joys and pleasures of the world': Mahadev Desai, *Day-to-day*, 2: 217.

53 I have been analysing my love: *CW,* 22:119.

56 do not hate, do not lust, do not hoard, do not kill, love your enemies: James D. Hunt, *Gandhi and the Nonconformists: Encounters in South Africa*, Promilla & Co., 1986, p. 42.

56 When I went to England, I was a votary of violence: *CW*, 43:5. Speech in Ahmedabad on Tolstoy's birth centenary, 10 September 1928 from Navajivan Publishing, 16 September 1928.

57 In the midst of death, life persists; in the midst of untruth: *Young India*, 11 October, 1928.

58 The greatest of things in this world are accomplished not through unaided human effort: Tendulkar, *Mahatma*, p. 291.

58 [God is] proving for me: M. K. Gandhi, *My Dear Child*, Ahmedabad: Navajivan Publishing, 1956, p. 106.

58 Just observe how God sustains me: Manu Gandhi, *Ekla Chalo Re*, pp. 91-92.

58 Today I find myself all alone: *CW*, 95:182-83

58 I embarked on the fast in the name of Truth: *CW*, 98:260-61

59 **You have said that Truth is God:** Vinoba Bhave, Bapu Paase (With Bapu) taken from Vinoba Bhave, *Ahimsa ni Khoj*, as published in Shashwat Gandhi, no. 39, Bhuj, Gujarat: Bhuj Aksharbharati Prakashan, September 2014, p. 9.

59 **A man who was completely innocent:** *CW*, 92: 345-46.

59 **Jesus Christ prayed to God:** *CW*, 97: 163

60 **it is better for India to discard violence altogether:** *Harijan*, 14 Oct 1939.

60 **let Hitler 'take possession of their land:** *Harijan*, 6 July 1940; *CW*, 78: 386-88.

61 **There was 'no doubt', Gandhi said:** *CW*, 97: 6-8.

CHAPTER 4: HIS VEXED RELATIONSHIP WITH CHURCHILL

62 **Suggesting that 'Asiatics' might 'teach the African natives evil ways':** Winston Churchill, *My African Journey*, London: The Holland Press, 1962, pp. 33-37.

63 **'striding half-naked up the steps of the viceregal palace':** David Hardiman, *Gandhi: In his Time and Ours*, New Delhi: Permanent Black, 2003, p. 238, citing Martin Gilbert, Winston Churchill, volume 5, p. 390.

63 **Congress had been 'raised to a towering pedestal':** Churchill's remark in the House of Commons on 12 March 1931 can be seen in *Winston Churchill: His Complete Speeches*, Robert Rhodes James (ed.), New York: Chelsea House, 1974, volume v (1928-1935), p. 4995.

63 **The object of our non-violent movement…is complete independence for India:** Mira Behn, *The Spirit's Pilgrimage*, London: Longmans Green, 1960, p. 143.

63 **'not become the King's First Minister in order to preside over the liquidation of the British Empire':** Churchill's broadcast of 24 August 1971 on the Atlantic Charter is in *Winston Churchill: His Complete Speeches*, volume vi, pp. 6472-6278. The 'King's First Minister' reference, in Churchill's remarks at the Lord Mayor's Luncheon on 10 November 1942, is in volume vi, p. 6695.

64 **'a peevish telegram to ask why Gandhi hadn't died yet.':** *Wavell: A Viceroy's Journal*, Penderel Moon (ed.), London: Oxford University Press, 1973, p. 79.

64 **'Pakistan, Hindustan and Princestan':** Ibid, p. 120 and 168.

64 **The fearful massacres which are occurring in India are no surprise to me:** Speech of 27 Sept 1947 to a Constituency Meeting in *Winston Churchill*, James (ed.), volume VII, pp. 7525-7526.

64 **called the former premier 'a great man'…prediction wrong:** *CW*, 97: 6-8.

66 **I cannot love Muslims or Hindus:** *Young India*, 6 August 1925.

66 **We cannot love one another:** *CW*, 36: 46

67 **I wish I were Commander-in-Chief in India…:** *The Letters of Charles Dickens*, Letter to Miss Burdett Coutts in Graham Story & Kathleen Tillotson

(eds.), Volume 8, 1856-58, Oxford: Clarendon Press, 1995, pp. 458-460.

67 **The colour of his beard, his eyebrows, his very lashes was yellower than the grapes:** Sheldon Pollock, 'Ramayana and Political Imagination in India,' *The Journal of Asian Studies 52*, no 2, May 1993, pp. 276-77.

68 **'They are all birds'... 'has his own convictions':** Entries for 27 March and 6 July 1932 in Mahadev Desai, *The Diary of Mahadev Desai*, 2 volumes, Ahmedabad: Navajivan Publishing, undated.

68 **a new and robust India:** *CW*, 90: 130.

68 **The extension of our rule over the whole Indian peninsula was made possible:** C.L.R. Fletcher and Rudyard Kipling, *A History of England*, Oxford: 1911, 1930 editions, p. 241.

69 **'complete indifference of the vast majority of the agricultural populations':** Ibid, p. 243.

71 **The hearts of most of us:** K. M. Munshi, *Pilgrimage to Freedom*, Bombay: Bhavan, 1967, pp. 16-17.

74 **In his superb sense of timing, in his quick intuitive grasp of the balance of forces:** George Woodcock, *Mohandas Gandhi*, New York: Penguin Viking, 1971, p. 61.

75 **To call woman the weaker sex is a libel:** *Young India*, 10 April 1930, 49: 57-9.

75 **Do you expect Purna Swaraj (Complete Independence) in your lifetime?:** Taken from Pattabhi Sitaramayya, *History of the Indian National Congress*, 1935-1947, Bombay: Padma, 1947, pp. 755-763.

77 **Seeing himself as a 'stifling' force:** *CW*, 64: 394-96.

78 **and a disconcerted Rajagopalachari argued that Gandhi would 'surely be disappointed':** Letters of 13 and 28 September, 1934, Devadas Gandhi Papers.

78 **It is not with a light heart:** *CW*, 64: 394-96

78 **I am not going out as a protest:** *CW*, 65: 212-3, 65: 229-30.

CHAPTER 5: THE LESSONS OF PARTITION

82 **'If one regiment mutinies, the next regiment [should be] so alien':** Letter from Wood Papers cited in S. R. Mehrotra, *The Emergence of the Indian National Congress*, New Delhi: Vikas Publishing, 1971, p. 105.

82 **I must send Your Excellency a line to say that a very:** Mary Elliot-Murray-Kynynmound, *Countess of Minto, India, Minto and Morley*, 1905-1910, London: Macmillan, 1934, p. 47.

86 **'I refuse to line up. There is a third party— the Muslims.':** Quoted in J. Ahmad, *Middle Phase of the Muslim Political Movement*, Lahore: Publishers United, 1969, p. 170.

86 **Whereas the ideologically-driven Jawaharlal Nehru:** *CW,* 26: 54, quoted in Malhotra, *Gandhi and the Punjab*, p. 115.

86 **However, in 1941, a vigilant viceroy and his officers in Lahore:** See Linlithgow to Hope, Governor of Madras, 8 May 1941, Linlithgow Papers,

London: India Office Library; Rajmohan Gandhi, *Rajaji: A Life*, New Delhi: Penguin, 1997, pp. 225-226.

87 **[I]n the midst of this catastrophe:** *CW*, 76: 312.

87 **a counter-check on Congress:** 1937 letter from Churchill to Linlithgow quoted in Bipan Chandra, *Communalism in Modern India*, New Delhi: Vikas Publishing, 1984, pp. 244-245; letter of 5 September 1939 from Linlithgow to Zetland in Chandra, *Communalism in Modern India*, p. 270.

87 **'It has been decided':** Linlithgow to George VI, Linlithgow Papers, 19 October 1939, London: India Office Library.

87 **'Up to the time of the declaration of war':** *Historic Documents of the Muslim Freedom Movement*, J. Ahmad (ed.), Lahore: Publishers United, p. 372.

88 **Jinnah 'blushed':** John Glendevon, *Viceroy at Bay*, London: Collins, 1971, p. 119.

88 **The Viceroy also asked Zafrulla Khan, a member of his executive council:** Wali Khan, *Facts Are Facts: The Untold Story of India's Partition*, New Delhi: Vikas Publishing, 1987, pp. 29-30.

88 **'separate and sovereign Muslim states, comprising geographically contiguous units':** A. H. Merriam, *Gandhi vs. Jinnah*, Calcutta: Minerva Associates, 1980, p. 67.

88 *The Times* **of London reported that prolonged cheering almost drowned Jinnah's remark:** Ibid, p. 66.

89 **If we say 'Punjab,' that would mean that the boundary of our state:** Quoted in *Iqbal, Jinnah and Pakistan*, C. M. Naim (ed.), Syracuse: Syracuse University, 1979, p. 186.

90 **It was India's historic destiny:** Arsh Malsian, *Abul Kalam Azad*, New Delhi: Publications Division, 1976.

90 **The 'Two Nations' theory is an untruth:** In October 1939 and April and May 1940. See *CW*, 77: 27; 78:109; and 79: 231.

90 **'worse than anarchy to partition a poor country like India':** Speech of 16 September 1940, *Harijan Sevak*, 12 October 1940; *CW*, 79: 231.

91 **If the vast majority of Indian Muslims feel that they are not one nation:** *Harijan*, 30 March 1940; *CW*, 78: 93.

91 **Pakistan cannot be worse than foreign domination:** *Harijan*, *CW*, 78: 178, 4 May 1940.

91 **The Muslims must have the same right of self-determination that the rest of India has:** *Harijan*, 6 April 1940; 78: 109.

91 **I do not say this as a Hindu:** Speech of 16 September 1940; *Harijan Sevak*, 79: 231, 12 October 1940.

91 **It also promised never to allow India's minorities:** *Collected Works*, 79: 466-468.

92 **Both were unwell, with amoebae bothering Gandhi:** Hector Bolitho, *Jinnah: Creator of Pakistan*, Connecticut: Greenwood Press, 1982, p. 148.

92 **'Let us call in a third party or parties to guide or even arbitrate between us':** *CW*, 84: 404.

94 **Later, Cripps would candidly tell the House of Commons:** House of

Commons Debates, 8 June 1946, quoted by S. R. Mehrotra, *The Partition of India*, C. H. Phillips and M. D. Wainwright (eds.), London: Allen and Unwin, 1970, p. 218.

94 **'as the first step on the road to Pakistan':** Nicholas Mansergh, *Transfer of Power 1942-7: The Mountbatten Viceroyalty, princes, partition, and independence, 8 July-15 August 1947*, Nicholas Mansergh, Esmond Walter Rawson Lumby, Penderel Moon (eds.), H. M. Stationery Office, 1983, 6: 684-7.

95 **claiming that 'the foundation of Pakistan' was 'inherent':** *Historic Documents*, Ahmad (ed.), pp. 522-523.

95 **'I must not act against my instinct':** Pyarelal, *Last Phase*, 1: 238-239.

95 **'I admit defeat. You are not bound to act upon my [advice]…':** Ibid, 1: 239.

96 **The Working Committee [members]:** *CW*, 91: 250.

97 **'to some form of Central Government':** Mansergh, *Transfer of Power*, 9: 729.

97 **On 8 March, pressed by Punjab's Sikh and Hindu leaders:** Ibid, 9: 901.

98 **When the Congress resolution was passed, Gandhi was in distant Bihar:** *CW*, 94: 153-54.

98 **Thirdly, Punjab's private bands should be disbanded:** For the text of his scheme that Gandhi left with the Viceroy on 4 April, see *CW*, 94: 229.

99 **I told [Azad] straightaway of Gandhi's plan:** Mansergh, *Transfer of Power*, 10: 86.

99 **[S]ome thirty-five minutes later, Mr. Jinnah:** Ibid, 10: 104.

99 **'basically Mr. Gandhi's objective was to retain the unity of India':** Ibid, 10: 84.

100 **'Tactics to be adopted with Gandhi as regards his scheme':** Ibid, 10: 129.

100 **I had several short talks with Pandit Nehru:** *CW*, 94: 283-84.

100 **that Gandhi's 'ill-conceived plan:** Entry dated 13 April 1947. Rajagopalachari Papers.

100 **Surely', Wolpert wrote, 'this was a King Solomon solution':** Stanley A. Wolpert, *Jinnah of Pakistan*, New York: Oxford University Press, 1984, p. 317.

CHAPTER 6: OF CASTE AND AMBEDKAR

102 **'There were no secrets between us. We exchanged our hearts every day':** *CW*, 83: 201-6.

102 **Recalling that Gandhi had 'again and again':** Andrews's letter quoted in *Gandhi and Charlie: The Story of a Friendship*, David M. Gracie, (ed.), Cambridge, Massachusetts: Cowley Publications, 1989, p. 155.

102 **Now for your important argument about untouchability:** *CW*, 61: 163-66.

103 **Thanks to these hypocritical distinctions:** *Indian Opinion*, 30 January 1909; *CW*, 9: 290-91.

104 **To a friend in southern India, Gandhi wrote that he had told Kasturba:** Letter to Srinivasa Sastri, *CW,* 15: 46, 23 September 1915.

104 **Santok fasted in opposition to the admission of Dudabhai:** *CW,* 15: 46.

104 **'washed their hearts clean of untouchability':** *CW,* 56: 178.

104 **Gandhi was thinking of moving the ashram:** M. K. Gandhi, *Autobiography: The Story of my Experiments with Truth,* New York: Dover Publications, 1983, pp. 356-57.

104 **Every affliction that we labour under:** 16 February 1916; *CW,* 15: 173.

104 **higher castes would become 'fit for Swaraj:** *CW,* 16: 135.

104 **When they tried to take water from a well next door:** Erikson, *Gandhi's Truth,* p. 299.

104 **'the movement for Swaraj will end in smoke' if 'untouchables':** *CW,* 22: 57, 5 December 1920.

105 **Gandhi answered that he would rather reject Swaraj than abandon the 'untouchables':** Remark quoted by Gandhi in *Young India,* 23 April and 4 May 1921; *CW,* 23: 46-47.

106 **I asked [Gandhi] repeatedly: why don't you hit out at the caste system directly?:** Tibor Mende, *Conversations with Nehru,* Bombay: Wilco, 1958, pp. 24-27.

107 **'even at the risk of getting his head broken':** *Young India,* 28 April 1927; *CW,* 33: 268.

107 **If we come into power with the stain of untouchability unaffected:** Pyarelal, p. 303.

108 **Sikhs may remain as such in perpetuity, so may [Muslims]:** *CW,* 48: 298.

108 **The 'untouchables' are in the hands of superior classes:** Ibid, 48: 258.

109 **'public wells, public schools, public roads and all other public institutions':** Ibid, 51: 159-60.

109 **Gandhi claimed during the fast that 'an increasing army of reformers':** Ibid, 51: 119.

110 **They could have taken up an uncompromising:** Ibid, 51: 143-145.

110 **The political part of [the settlement]:** Ibid.

110 **I did expect a mighty response from the orthodox:** Ibid, 51: 154.

111 **'When the fast failed and Mr. Gandhi was obliged to sign a pact':** Dr. B. R. Ambedkar, *What Congress and Gandhi Have Done to the Untouchables,* Bombay: Thacker and Co., 1945.

112 **When caste Hindus realized their folly and repented:** *CW,* 53: 266–267.

112 **If to relegate a body of people to distant locations:** *Harijan,* 25 Feb 1933; *CW,* 53: 405.

113 **The fight against sanatanists is becoming more and more interesting:** *CW,* 53: 309–10.

113 **If this doctrine of utmost superiority:** *CW,* 59: 275.

114 **When a huge earthquake destroyed towns and villages in north Bihar in January 1934:** *CW,* 63: 38-40.

114 'hold [Gandhi] and his followers responsible for the visitation of Divine anger': *CW,* 63: 516.

114 [W]hilst we have yet breathing time, let us get rid of the distinctions of high and low: *CW,* 63: 40.

114 'untouchability has become weak and limp': Remark to Ashram colleagues, Patna, 22 March 1934; *CW,* 63: 305.

115 'Did Kasturba really enter the temple?': Narayan Desai, *Bliss Was It To Be Young With Gandhi,* Bombay: Bhavan, 1988, p. 44.

116 From the late 1930s, Gandhi blessed marriages between Dalits and non-Dalits: Nishikant Kolge discusses this question in detail in his unpublished thesis on *Gandhi and Caste,* pp. 139-145.

117 Who are the people who beat up Harijans, murder them: *CW,* 85: 102.

117 Invite a Harijan every day to dine with you: *CW,* 93: 229.

117 'made it a rule...to be present or give his blessings': *CW,* 87: 350.

118 According to Khairmode, Ambedkar gave an encouraging response: Khairmode quoted in M. S. Gore, *The Social Context of an Ideology: Ambedkar's Political and Social Thought,* New Delhi: Sage Publications, 1993, pp. 180-181.

118 'Dr. Ambedkar was good enough to attend the Assembly': *CW,* 86: 426.

118 Another Ambedkar associate, Roshanlal Shastri, has written that: Roshanlal Shastri, *Babasaheb Dr. Ambedkar Ke Sampark Me 25 Varsh,* 3rd edition, New Delhi: Buddhist Society of India, pp. 32-33.

119 They have not become our enemies: *CW,* 96: 147-48

119 'I am sure if Bapu were alive he would have given you his blessings': *CW,* 6: 302.

120 'I feel like crying over his death': *CW,* 95: 179.

120 [T]he time is fast approaching when India will have to elect: *CW,* 95: 193.

120 If all the leaders join the Cabinet: *CW,* 95: 217.

121 [I]f I have my way: *CW,* 95: 417-418.

121 Gandhi agreed to Mountbatten staying on: *CW,* 96: 174.

121 In his 14 June speech to the AICC in which he conveyed his acquiescence to partition: *CW,* 88: 155-56; 95: 286-7.

122 It is a matter of shame for us that there are: *CW,* 97: 378.

122 'How are the Harijans?' he asked the higher-caste leaders: *CW,* 98: 340.

CHAPTER 7: AHIMSA AND GANDHI

123 Gandhi wished 'to liberate India': Fischer quoted in Francis Watson and Hallam Tennyson (eds.), *Talking of Gandhi,* Calcutta: Orient Longman, 1957, p. 37.

124 For a bowl of water give a goodly meal: Gandhi, *Autobiography,* p. 31.

125 As a coward, which I was for years, I harboured violence: *Young India,* 29 May 1924; *CW,* 28: 50.

125 'Having flung aside the sword, there is nothing except the cup of love': *Young India*, 2 April 1931.

126 'Never again,' he told himself, would he be caught in a 'false': Gandhi, *Autobiography*, p. 86.

127 The next morning it was with difficulty that Gandhi managed: Ibid, pp. 99-104.

127 'independent thinking, profound morality and truthfulness' in Tolstoy's presentation: Ibid, p. 120.

128 The Sepoy War was quelled by means of superior force: *CW,* 94: 111.

128 [W]e are nurturing attitudes: *CW,* 96: 129-30.

130 'So far and wide have the roots of Japanese victory spread': *Indian Opinion*, 28 October 1905; *CW,* 4: 470-471.

130 Two, Gandhi's close reading of Henry David Thoreau's 'classic' essay: *Collected Works*, 7: 429, where Gandhi refers to Thoreau's 'Resistance to Civil Government (Civil Disobedience).

130 'one of the greatest and most moral men America has produced': *Indian Opinion*, 26 October 1907; *CW,* 7: 279.

132 No man can claim to be absolutely in the right: M. K. Gandhi, *Hind Swaraj and Other Writings*, Anthony Parel (ed.), Cambridge, UK: Cambridge University Press, 2003, p. 91.

132 'Even a man weak in body is capable of offering this resistance': Gandhi, *Hind Swaraj*, p. 94.

132 We cannot win Swaraj for our famishing millions: Remarks in 1931 in *CW,* 51: 301, 316-17.

133 War demoralizes those who are trained for it: Ibid, 10: 159.

134 Read this. Chew the end: Desai, Day-to-day, volume 1, pp. 2-3.

134 In spite of the negative particle: *CW,* 68: 198-202.

135 I used to be a tyrant at home: *CW,* 74: 147.

138 that to compel 'a single person' to shout nationalist slogans: Ibid, 90: 4-6.

138 Outwardly we followed truth and non-violence: Ibid, 96: 129.

139 That black pall of fear was lifted from the people's shoulders: Jawaharlal Nehru, *Discovery of India*, New Delhi: Oxford University Press, 1989, pp. 358-359.

139 No one at the time: *CW,* 95: 289.

140 If there is the slightest communal taint: *CW,* 83: 181-85.

141 No underreported story can be greater or nobler than this one: Rajmohan Gandhi, *Punjab: A History from Aurangzeb to Mountbatten*, 1707-1947, New Delhi: Aleph Book Company, 2013.

142 It is painful to [read this]: Remark on 25 December ; *CW,* 90: 297.

142 They killed him, this man who had galvanized 400 million [Indians] for independence...: *The Papers of Martin Luther King, Jr.*, Berkeley: University of California Press, 1992, volume 5, p. 156.

CHAPTER 8: THE LAST DAYS OF GANDHI

144 'They bathe us with love': Manu Gandhi, *Ekla Chalo Re*, p. 108.

144 'A house full of love, such as this one': Tendulkar, *Mahatma*, 7: 373.

145 'daily ministrations on behalf of love': Bose, *My Days with Gandhi*, Calcutta: Nishana, 1953, p. 8 and Bose, *Lectures on Gandhism*, Ahmedabad: Navajivan Publishing, 1971, p. 65.

145 After the women left, he said to Manu that their faces would haunt him: Manu Gandhi, *Ekla Chalo Re*, p. 69.

145 'We don't go to our temples, mosques or churches with shoes on': Ibid, p. 54.

145 'The pitch of Gandhi's [own] voice was low, but the tune was correct': Tendulkar, *Mahatma*, 7: 355.

145 On 31 January, Muslims in Navagram defended Gandhi's right: Ibid, 7: 382.

145 When a maulvi said that Hindus willing to convert: Bose, *My Days with Gandhi*, pp. 149-150.

146 There is the One...above all of us who will look after me: Manu Gandhi, *Ekla Chalo Re*, p. 55.

146 'Where people don't have twigs for baking their rotis': Ibid, pp. 111-112.

146 'On this day, and exactly at this time, Ba quitted her mortal': *CW*, 94: 13.

147 'questioning attitude towards his own perfection': Bose, *Lectures on Gandhism*, p. 63.

147 Yes, that is true of the Poet, for he has to bring down the light: Ibid, pp. 105-106.

147 In Bhatialpur, Muslims pledged that they would risk their lives: *CW*, 93: 278.

147 Eleven Muslims of Sirandi took the pledge, 'with God as witness': Pyarelal, *Last Phase*, 1: 515.

148 Gandhi replied that 'it was to save them from that sin': Ibid, 1: 622.

148 killings in his province were 'like the Jallianwala massacre': Ibid.

148 Is it or is it not a fact: *CW*, 94: 147-48.

149 The Hindus of Bihar: Ibid, 94: 75-6.

149 Abducted women, stolen goods and illegal arms should be returned: Pyarelal, *Last Phase*, 1: 666.

149 After the prayer address, Gandhiji stayed on to collect money: Ibid, 1: 661.

150 I am very sorry to learn that you got the articles on Wednesday: *Harijan*, *CW*, 96: 254-255.

150 I will give you a talisman: See plate opposite page 89, with the text in English and Gandhi's signature in English and Bengali, in Tendulkar, *Mahatma*, Bombay, volume 8.

151 Abha and Manu, 'two very brave girls': *CW*, 96: 315.

151 'I pin my hopes on you two': *CW,* 96: 313.

151 sees 'two dead bodies of very poor Muslims': *CW,* 96: 317; Green, *Gandhi,* p. 378.

151 In the afternoon a telegram arrives from Nehru: *CW,* 96: 321fn.

151 'Can you fast against *goondas?*': *CW,* 96: 318.

152 Some [university students]... gathered weapons from streets and homes: Amiya Chakravarty quoted in Gene Sharp, *Gandhi Wields the Weapon of Moral Power,* Ahmedabad: Navajivan Publishing, 1960, pp. 259-260.

152 'the saint, the martyr and the virgin, [working] together': Green, *Gandhi,* p. 240.

152 'Gandhiji has achieved many things': *The Statesman,* Calcutta, 6 September 1947.

153 'localities like Karol Bagh, Sabzimandi and Paharganj were being emptied of Muslims': Brij Krishna, *Gandhiji ki Dilli Diary,* Delhi: Gandhi Smarak Nidhi and Gyamdeep, 1970, volume 3, p. 278.

153 For a 'whole day long' he listened 'to the tale of woe that [was] Delhi': *CW,* 96: 352.

152 'had not undergone the hardships that they [had]...': Ibid, 96: 357.

154 Gandhi's hosts at Birla House said the city was in such disarray: Ibid, 96: 356.

154 'If Gandhiji had waited some more days before coming to Delhi': Krishna, *Gandhiji ki Dilli Diary,* volume 3, p. 382.

154 Two days after Gandhi's arrival in Delhi, the US military: Nisid Hajari, *Midnight's Furies: The Deadly Legacy of India's Partition,* New York: Houghton Mifflin Harcourt, 2015, p. 157, citing 'Letter from Macdonald to Marshall' in US: 845.00/9-1147.

154 '[T]here was no assurance that either police or Indian Army troops will interfere': Ibid, p. 159, citing US: 845.00/9-1847.

154 Three days after reaching Delhi, Gandhi confronted the: Krishna, *Dilli Diary,* 3: 287, and letter of 27 October 1948 from Nehru to Patel in Durga Das (ed.), *Sardar Patel's Correspondence,* Ahmedabad: Navajivan Publishing, volume 7, p. 672.

155 'How can a sinner claim the right to judge or execute another sinner?': Krishna, *Dilli Diary,* 3: 294-297.

156 I have just a handful of bones in my body: *CW,* 96: 418-419.

156 Far from losing your desire to live until you are 125: Ibid, 97: 204.

156 I am not vain enough to think that the divine purpose: *CW,* 97: 39

156 I look after my health with care: Ibid, 97: 251.

157 I saw your letter only now: Ibid, 97: 221.

157 Dear Lord Mountbatten, This little thing is made out of doubled yarn: Ibid, 97: 265.

157 My physician today, in my thought: Ibid, 97: 257.

158 We must kindle the light of love within: Ibid, 90: 18.

158 My Raam is not a man with two hands and two feet: Ibid, 97: 343.

158 If...you want to go of your own will: Ibid, 97: 443.

158 Gandhi remarked:'Today not everybody can move about freely': Pyarelal, *Last Phase*, 2: 697.

159 'for making bullets to be shot at us': *Sardar Patel Centenary*, v olume 2, G. M. Nandurkar (ed.), Ahmedabad: Sardar Vallabhbhai Patel Smarak Bhavan, 1975, p. 19.

159 On 11 January he was shaken afresh when a group of Delhi's Muslims: Pyarelal, *Last Phase*, 2: 700-701.

159 'on the sun-drenched spacious Birla House lawn': Ibid, 2: 701.

159 Though the voice within has been beckoning: 98: 218-220.

160 You have surrendered to impatience...: Pyarelal, *Last Phase*, 2: 704.

160 A 'very much upset' Vallabhbhai Patel offered to resign: Entry of 12 January 1948 in *The Diary of Maniben Patel,* Prabha Chopra (ed.), New Delhi: Vision Books, 2002.

160 Delhi is the capital of India: 98: 229-235.

161 'by Muslim women in the seclusion of their purda': Pyarelal, *Last Phase*, 2: 713-14.

161 'live and work for the cause of Hindu-Muslim unity in the two dominions': Jehangir Patel and Marjorie Sykes, *Gandhi: His Gift of the Fight*, Rasulia, Madhya Pradesh: Friends Rural Centre, 1987, p. 188.

162 The poet says, 'If there is Paradise: *CW*, 98: 234-235.

162 We take the pledge that we shall protect: Ibid, 98: 253.

163 he spoke for the Hindu Mahasabha: Ibid, 98: 253-7.

163 Brij Krishna thought that Gandhi's shrunken and lined face looked radiant: Krishna, *Dilli Diary*, 3: 576-81.

CHAPTER 9: THE ENDURING TRUTH IN HIS WRITINGS

166 As Anthony Parel points out, *Hind Swaraj* permits the use of force: M. K. Gandhi, *Hind Swaraj*, Anthony J. Parel (ed.), New Delhi: Cambridge University Press, 1997, p. 86fn.

167 'HE SHAN'T MOVE AN INCH,' said the voice: Prabhudas Gandhi, *Jeevan Prabhat*, New Delhi: Sasta Sahitya Mandal Prakashan, 1954, pp. 197-198.

169 'an Empire in which he was not to be trusted...': *CW*, 9: 508-10.

169 Will you press for Purna Swaraj: *CW*, 51: 220-23, 6 March 1931.

170 my eyes water and my throat gets parched': *Hind Swaraj*, Anthony J. Parel (ed.), p. 42.

170 Stop to welcome him, from close quarters sitting in boats: Quoted by Akhtarul Wasey in *History, Culture and Society in India and West Asia*, N. N. Vohra (ed.), New Delhi: Shipra Publications, 2003, p. 281.

171 In his letter Gandhi first referred to divide-and-rule and to 'the initial mistake of the British being': *CW*, 95: 348.

171 To them I would respectfully say...: *Hind Swaraj*, pp. 113-114.

172 Where shall I go and where shall I take the forty crores of India?: *CW*, 83: 201-206.

174 If all the British were to be killed, those who kill them: 1908 statement,

8: 374, quoted in *Hind Swaraj*, p. 78fn.

174 **Even should the British leave in consequence of such murderous acts:** *Indian Opinion*, 14 August 1909.

174 **How can the millions obtain self-rule?:** *Hind Swaraj*, pp. 76-77.

174 **One's head bends before Bhagat Singh's bravery:** *CW,* 51: 301.

175 **'My patriotism does not teach me that I am to allow people to be crushed':** *Hind Swaraj*, pp. 77-78.

175 **When individuals who are 'intensely dissatisfied with the present pitiable:** In the invaluable Hind Swaraj volume that he has edited (Cambridge, 1997), Anthony Parel suggests (116fn) that this refers to dissatisfaction with modernity. It is equally or more likely that dissatisfaction with Empire was implied.

175 **'they will not cower before brute force and will not':** Ibid, p. 116.

175 **It was more courageous 'with a smiling face to approach':** Ibid, p. 93.

175 **A satyagrahi 'will say he will not obey:** *Ibid*, p. 91.

175 **Even a man weak in body:** Ibid, p. 94.

176 **Do you think that all the women and the children:** *CW***,** 51: 305-309.

176 **'No man can claim to be absolutely in the right':** *Hind Swaraj*, p. 91.

176 **brute force is not natural to the Indian soil:** Ibid, p. 112.

177 **When I see... the views of Indian nationalists:** *Indian Opinion*, 8 January 1910, 10: 107-110.

177 **When I was in detention in the Aga Khan Palace:** *Harijan, CW,* 93:43, 8 December 1946,

178 **'deliver the message of unadulterated non-violence to the world':** *CW,* 62: 202.

178 **'Not one hair of one head of one white person shall be harmed':** Bayard Rustin, *Down the Line*, Chicago: Quadrangle Books, 1971, p. 103.

179 **In [the] village of my dreams:** The discussion can be seen in *CW,* 88: 118-20, 329-31.

179 **Society is made up of individuals. It is we that make society...:** Ibid, 98: 234-235.

179 **'Many examples can be given in which acts of majorities':** *Hind Swaraj*, p. 92.

180 **Let everyone become his own walking newspaper:** *Harijan*, 3 November 1940; *CW,* 79: 330.

180 **If you want real freedom:** *CW,* 83: 181-185.

181 **In this structure composed of innumerable villages:** Ibid, 91: 325-327.

182 **'the dazzling and bright surface of modern civilization':** *CW,* 1: 185, 3 December 1894.

182 **'a civilization [whose] greatest achievement':** Ibid, 1: 206.

182 **'the tinsel splendour of modern civilization':** Ibid, 3: 209.